RICE PAPER WINDOW

CHRISTABEL CHOI

Cover design by Christabel Choi

Published by Paper Angel Press
paperangelpress.com

ISBN 978-1-967547-61-6 (Trade Paperback)

FIRST EDITION

10 9 8 7 6 5 4 3 2 1

For my parents
Warren and Robin Hudson

RICE
PAPER
WINDOW

PROLOGUE

I N THE LATE 1980s, the whole world was changing, including Korea. I was a student at Yonsei University, where my housemates and classmates were actively dismantling authoritarian rule and ushering in democracy. I lived in a historic traditional home in a temple, at a time when such houses were disappearing. Realizing I was present at a historic moment, I kept a careful journal. This memoir is focused on 1989, compiled from my contemporary notes.

The title of this book is inspired by a 1973 book by another American in Korea, Michael J Daniels of Sogang University, who said that although foreigners cannot see Korea clearly—as if we are looking through "A Rain-Spattered Window"—we gain a great richness in making the effort.

FEBRUARY 1989

1

KIMPO AIRPORT, SOUTH KOREA CUSTOMS

I ARRIVE AT KIMPO AIRPORT in the cold, damp February of 1989. Kim Il Sung is the Supreme Leader of North Korea. George Bush has just been inaugurated as President of the United States. South Korea has successfully hosted the 1988 Olympics. Despite violently suppressing demonstrations, the dictator Chun Doo Hwan was recently forced to step down to make way for the first democratically elected Korean president in decades: Roh Tae Woo. The country is still trying to find its footing as a democracy and students are still leading the protests for reform. I am twenty years old, enrolled for a semester at the Yonsei University Graduate School of International Studies in the capital city of Seoul.

The plane has not even entered Korean airspace when I have my first reminder that this country is not quite a democracy. Civil war is still simmering between north and south. I am a student of Russian language and history, so brought along a copy of the Communist Manifesto to prepare for my Soviet Studies class. When I take the book out of my purse the passenger seated next to me quietly tells me to put it away, out of sight. I hadn't thought about the danger of my reading list. Simple possession of the Manifesto could land me in a South Korean jail. Even in the past two years, I have heard that Korean students died in police custody just for the accusation that they might have communist or North Korean sympathies, basically to fill quotas so that the government could look like it was doing something, I guess, about the communist threat.

Gathering our bags from the overhead racks, we passengers slowly file out of the airplane and head for Passport Control. We walk between rows of tall, motionless military guards—motionless but for their eyes, which I feel tracking me below the brims of hats they wear pulled low over their eyebrows. I worry that they might have x-ray vision and see the forbidden Manifesto now hidden in my bag.

After passing the gauntlet of guards, trying to keep my breath and heartbeat steady, I join the foreigner's line for Korean Customs. *Customs*. I've been looking forward to spending the next eight months passing through Korean culture and customs, until they are etched into my movement, speech, and memory. The official at the counter today simply stamps my passport and without a smile, welcomes me to Korea. I pass through to baggage claim and breathe a sigh of relief.

Retrieving my backpack from the carousel, I realize we have yet to present our bags for inspection. My line leads to a low platform where I lay down my bag in front of a young, blue-uniformed customs officer. I had forgotten this part of the process and, casually so as not to draw attention, I push the strap on my shoulder so the handbag hangs less visible behind me. The customs officer motions for me to unclip the straps on my luggage. He opens it to examine the contents. I remember that, at the last minute, I stuffed in a box of sanitary napkins. The official looks at the squashed box on top of my clothes, perplexed, then asks me what it is. I look at the floor and mumble, "sanitary pads."

To my embarrassment, he holds up the box and loudly asks me again, "What is this?" I hold my breath and, hesitantly, reach out to take the box, slowly turning it over to point out the diagram on back which shows graphic instructions of how to place a pad in underwear. I hand it back. The young official stares curiously at the diagram for a moment, then gasps and drops the box so suddenly it almost falls to the floor. I lurch forward to catch it and stuff it into my handbag on top of my books. Hearing laughter from the other agents, I look up. His face is bright red, and he hastily closes my backpack, waving me on while the other agents continue teasing him.

In the confusion, he has forgotten—or is too embarrassed—to check my handbag, missing my forbidden copy of the Manifesto. I make a mental note to myself: for faster and safer customs control, pack sanitary products on top.

2

WELCOME TO KOREA

F INISHED WITH BAGGAGE CLAIM and customs at last, we passengers roll our carts out through opaque glass sliding doors into a sea of waiting friends, relatives, and drivers holding welcome signs for guests. Everyone in the crowd looks Korean but for the two pale, expectant faces of my parents, and I make a beeline for them.

This is my third time in Korea. The first time I flew in was the summer after my first year of college. As the plane approached Kimpo Airport, I had looked out over the verdant green countryside and rice paddies and felt an overwhelming sense of returning home—home to this place that felt achingly familiar, though I'd never been here before. It feels good to be back yet again.

Dad catches a taxi at the curb outside. Mom and I follow with the bags. The driver puts them into the trunk, and I settle in the back seat with my mother, relieved to be safely away from the authorities at the airport. Dad gets in front, next to the driver.

Our taxi driver zips away from the airport, weaving around pedestrians with giant roller bags, and out into the landscape of rice paddies I'd seen from the plane. Passing them now, we can see shining white egrets posing against the bright green of the fields.

Before long, we pass through the suburban outskirts of Seoul: rows of towering gray high-rise apartments, each marked with a specific number and letter, but otherwise looking the same, each apartment with a large window and balcony.

Soon we enter the city, where the driver swerves and honks through the tangled traffic. My mother and I grab hands and hold our breath as he miraculously squeezes the taxi between merging buses without a scratch. We exhale in relief, but don't let go of each other's hands.

I stare out the smog-spotted window onto a scene of more gray cement and dull, square buildings contrasting with colorful signs and the busy activity of brightly dressed women and men. Children of all sizes are playing on the sidewalks, bundled up against the cold in thick jackets and quilted pants. Babies are strapped to their mothers' backs in multi-colored blankets tied securely around both mother and child. Lots of primary colors along with pinks and greens.

I love this city. Despite the demonstrations, the smog, and the turbulent politics—or partly because of them (except the smog)—the vibrant character of Seoul has captured my heart.

Korea is a country very proud of its ancient culture and history but is also moving rapidly and intentionally into the future. The rapid changes are evident in every visit. This time, I have already noticed that there are more cars on the road, some of them ordinary private cars, which I barely saw any of two years ago.

My parents moved here when I started college, so their apartment in Seoul is my home address. They live in the English-speaking world of the Foreign School compound, a small drop of an American world in Korea. My parents are restless, though, and travel in Korea at every opportunity.

I have explored Seoul together with them, and sometimes on my own, especially the palaces and markets, but we have also gone south to Jeju Island and the beautiful historical city of Kyongju, my favorite. I have watched and listened carefully to pick up what little I could about Korean language and etiquette, but my vocabulary still consists of mainly numbers and a few greetings.

My hair is a bright yellow flag labeling me as foreign, and draws attention from passengers in other vehicles—attention I can't ignore. The stares that return my own wide-eyed curiosity remind me that we are the unusual ones. I sense what it feels like to be one of my sisters, being the one who looks different from almost everyone else in our town. A car stops next to us, far too short of the traffic light, the astonished driver staring at me until the light turns green and our taxi pulls ahead of his car. A woman in another car jumps in shock as our eyes meet. She gasps, and I see her exclaiming "Ommo!" Children watch us, wide-eyed, until we are out of sight.

3

LANGUAGE

THE STREET SIGNS and shop signs are all in Korean, of course. I try to sound out the words. I studied *Hangul*, the Korean alphabet, in my free time on a prior visit. The phonetic symbols of Korea's blocky letters are fairly easy to learn, and I can slowly make out syllables, but the vocabulary is too different from English for me to figure out. I can barely even recognize "English" words, spelled syllable by syllable according to Korean pronunciation.

The syllables are divided differently than in English, and I realize that some Korean letters do not even exist in English, just as some English letters do not exist in Korean. When an English word has sounds not distinguished in the Korean alphabet, the default is the closest phonetic equivalent. I realize *Pija* is "Pizza" and *khom-pyu-toh* is "computer." We are riding in a *tak-shi*.

Since the consonant and vowel sounds do not correspond perfectly, the same English letter might be represented differently in different Korean words. I try to figure out T and D; G, C and K; P and B. Similarly, we don't have a letter that exactly represents a Korean sound I hear as half 'p' and half 'b.' The map I'm holding labels the second largest city in South Korea, a port at the southern tip, as *Pusan* in English, but the map at the airport read *Busan*. On both maps, the Korean text reads the same, of course. The transliteration into Latin letters has not yet been standardized.

Korean words connect consonants differently than in English, and rarely end in a hard consonant. They seem to add a vowel sound at the ends of foreign words that do.

My mother wants to pick up a treat for me on the way home, and fearlessly sets to work preparing to ask the taxi driver if we can stop at a corner shop for ice cream before we head up the hill to the school. My parents must eat it only when I am here because she has to look the word up in her dictionary.

Ice cream is one of the first words I learn in a language, and I'm pretty sure the word in Korean is the same as in English. No, Mom insists, and very carefully sounds out the string of syllables. My father and I laugh when we hear her: "*Ah-ee-suh Ku-ree-muh*!" Ice cream. Of course.

The different alphabet makes my parents feel it is impossible for foreigners to learn to read Korean, but the pronunciation is more reliable than in English, and objectively one of the easiest scripts to learn. I practice by reading aloud any words I see, and can pick out some common words. To be fair, Korean really is one of the most difficult languages for Americans to learn—not because of the alphabet, but because our vocabulary and grammar are so different, not to mention the different levels of respect, age, and gender relationship.

4

BOARDING HOUSE

THIS FIRST COUPLE OF WEEKS, I am staying with my parents in their apartment on Seoul Foreign School campus. Even apartments for foreigners in Korea tend to be of less than generous proportions by American standards, and the one in which my parents live is no exception. It consists of two small bedrooms, a living room which doubles as a dining area, a bathroom, and a kitchen, each just large enough to be serviceable, and no more. The second bedroom has no western bed frame, so I lay out my bedroll at night and tri-fold the blankets and mattress in the morning.

We are all getting along well for now, but these tight quarters will become tighter next month when my classes begin and I need a place to study. I could stay in the international dorm on campus, but I would really rather live in a Korean dorm, if I can. Among the housing options, apparently, are student boarding houses. The university doesn't help with finding private housing, so it is hard for foreigners to find. Luckily, I have a lead on one. It's at a Buddhist temple nearby.

A friend of a friend of a friend—a Korean-American woman who is here to study art—is returning to America. She currently lives in a room behind the university in the Bongweon-sa (*sa* means temple) compound. I was surprised to learn that they rent out rooms, but she explains that some of the monks of this Zen order at Bongweon Temple are married, so the compound includes extensive housing for families. The modern family is smaller than the traditional one and there are fewer monks than there used to be, so several of the homes have empty rooms that the families let out to boarders, often students.

Bongweon Temple is home to some of the Living National Treasures of Buddhist art, dance, and music. The Artist has been studying Buddhist painting there. She gives me a tour of the temple, including an introduction to her teacher, Living National Treasure Man-Bong Sunim (monk) who is preparing a painting—the paper on which he is working covers the entire floor of a room in his house. He acknowledges our greeting with a nod and a smile, then returns to his work.

As we watch him, she explains how this style involves drawing a wall-sized template of religious scenes or designs, then transferring the image onto a painting surface by sifting powder through pinholes pierced along the lines of the original drawing. Then, sitting on the paper surface itself, the Artist paints the resulting cartoon. We watch for a while as he brings the painting to life in an elaborate display of sweeping swirls and bold figures in layers of bright colors.

My Artist guide is heading back to the States next week. She agrees to introduce me to the head monk of the side temple—actually an older, independent temple adjacent to the larger temple—where she lives, and to his wife. If they accept me, maybe I can rent her empty room when she leaves next week.

We meet and they quietly assess me, then agree I can move into their home as soon as the room is free and after the rain lets up. I will be so glad to have a place for myself. The rooms in the temple are quiet and peacefully traditional— small, but with the heated floors and the latticed, rice paper sliding doors of the old-style houses. I will have no choice but to progress in learning Korean: the monks and their families, even the students in the boarding house, do not speak much English, if at all.

The courtyard of this particular house opens onto a stairway to the temple buildings. The door to the room I hope to live in faces these stairs and, following a border of bushes to the top, I can see the latticed doors and winged roof of Yongam "Dragon Rock" Temple; and when we climb the stairs, we also find a smaller temple for the Mountain Spirit, which houses a painting of a smiling old man sitting casually with a tiger.

As we are about to leave, we run into a young monk of the temple in the courtyard, catching him as he gets ready to go out. He is throwing his arms into the sleeves of his grey monk's jacket which flaps around his shoulders like a bird, fluttering and settling into place. He is slightly older than us, and has a startlingly open personality. After meeting the peacefully dignified older men, he is a whirlwind by comparison.

He smiles broadly when he sees us and extends his hand in greeting. No one else has offered to shake hands when we meet. Most people bow, so I am startled at his outstretched hand. I hesitate, then bow as I shake his hand. He laughs joyfully, picks up his grey monk's bag, and heads out the gate to wherever he is going.

The Artist tells me more about him. He is a student monk who was given to the temple as a child and is now being groomed to be the next head of this temple. Apparently, he was an orphan. I am surprised, because he is so happy and carefree, none of the solemnity of the head monk, his adopted father. She tells me he is also training with the Living National Treasure of Buddhist Dance and Chanting.

5

NAMING

WHAT TO CALL PEOPLE? It's complicated. In Korea we don't use first names the way we do in the U.S. Even the term "first name" doesn't make sense, because names are written with family name first (one syllable), followed by a personal name (usually two syllables). Sometimes you will find someone with only a one-syllable personal name or very occasionally you'll meet someone with an ancient style Korean name with more syllables. Like in any culture, nothing is absolute, just general. But it's pretty solid that you don't just call someone older by their first name. That's way too intimate and thus disrespectful.

Relative age and gender are important, so you should start by learning how to call an elder *haraboji* (grandfather) or *halmoni* (grandmother). This refers to your social relationship, but is the same for family. Someone your parents' age, but not related, would be *ajeossi* (uncle) or *ajumoni* (auntie).

For someone close to your own age, how to address them is a little more complicated. It is totally okay, even expected, to ask someone who looks your own age how old they are so you don't use the wrong address. That's not rude, it's necessary in order to know the register with which to converse with the person.

If speaking with or referring to someone a little older, the easiest thing to do, if you know their personal name, is to add *-ssi* (sounds like shi) to the end. That's just polite. But sometimes it's not easy to learn someone's personal name because everyone usually just calls them "older brother" or "older sister," and you don't hear their first name used. As a younger person, it could be awkward to ask. To make it more complex, the way you say older brother or sister differs depending on whether you, yourself, are a younger "brother" or a younger "sister". Like with grandparents, the term can mean a family member, or not.

For someone clearly younger, you can just call them "*dongsaeng*" (younger sibling) but when they are younger you can actually just ask and use their personal name.

Fellow students can use *seonbae* or *hubae* to refer to one another as "senior" or "junior", respectively, to oneself. Or one can refer to some special trait, which is what I do in my journal because I can't just write "older brother" or "older sister" and keep everyone straight on the page. Even in conversation, I could say, "the soccer player" for example, referring to someone who is obsessed with soccer, and everyone would know who I mean. The more I learn, however, the more complex I realize the language is.

My parents have a friend I call "the Teacher". He's a few years older than me, and not a student. He's a teacher, so that's what I call him in Korean. Calling him by his first name with -*ssi*, or calling him "older brother" feels a bit too informal, so I use his professional title. It's correct, keeps the proper distance, but is also personal, in a way, because teachers take care of students, and students rely on teachers. There's more nuance, but it all works.

6

TEMPLE

THE TEMPLE ROOM is now prepared, and I can move there soon—after the rain lets up for a while. The path from the temple parking lot to my new house is slick and muddy, and it will be difficult to move my things until it dries out a bit.

MARCH 1, 1989

—

MARCH 14, 1989

7

REINTRODUCTION

THE TEACHER finds out I haven't explored the city much, even though I have been here twice before. Since I'm in college most of the year I can usually only come during vacations: summer and winter. This is the first time I'll be here in the springtime.

The first time I came to Korea, in the summer of 1987, the country was in the midst of overthrowing the dictatorship so although we managed to do some touring, the streets were often closed off due to police blockades, with rows and rows of armored police buses and riot police lining the streets, not to mention the persistent sting of tear gas.

When I came for Christmas, it was so cold the wind felt like it was blowing right through my bones. Last summer I couldn't come for the Olympics because I was in Russian summer school, and I couldn't come in the winter because I was on a research vessel at sea. This time I intend to stay until fall, at least.

The Teacher offers to guide me around the city to reintroduce me to the life of Seoul—as a resident, not a tourist. He is both Korean and American, and shows me the city through the eyes of both cultures. In a single day, I learn more about Korea than in all my previous visits combined.

We catch a bus at the front gate of the University and go to the national Kyongbok Palace, Biwon (Secret Garden), Insa-dong (*dong* means district) of antiques and arts markets, Lotte Department Store, and Namdae-mun (*nam* is south, *dae* is great, *mun* is gate) Market—destinations which make me happily dizzy with their vibrant activity and endless variety. Anything you need to buy, you can probably find at Namdae-mun. Although I have been to many of these places as a foreign tourist, I realize I have never actually *seen* them until now. And we are seen, too. He gets almost as many stares for being with me as I usually get all by myself.

With the Teacher guiding me, confusions and foreignness begin to resolve themselves in my spinning mind, slowly settling into clearer order. In small lunch spots, we eat rice cake soups (*ddok-guk*) and fried dumplings (*gun-mandu*) that are standard lunch foods in Korea, but that I have never tasted before. I've mostly had only the mixed rice and vegetables dish, *bibimpap,* that the other new foreigners order. We talk about Korean points of view, and he teaches me some words and phrases, insisting I buy the tickets to the palace and museum by myself—in Korean. I practice, reciting it over and over under my breath, then quickly forget as soon as I've used it. But I know the words will come more easily the next time I learn them.

When I visited these places with other foreigners two years ago, I simply saw the exotic: upswept rooflines, fiercely dramatic animal statues at Kyongbok-kung (*Kung* means palace); and at Insa-dong, the shop windows lined with rows of impossibly huge paint brushes, sets of brass bowls, statuettes, calligraphy, pink quilted pillows, and blankets too thick to sleep under. The bright colors and patchwork, floral, or striped designs were pretty, but I didn't understand their purpose. Not knowing there was so much I didn't know, I had simply enjoyed the pageantry. Now the shell is cracking, and with the Teacher's encouragement I begin to see inside the personality of this loud and colorful city.

Kyongbok-kung is a scaled down version of the old Royal Palace of Korea, with many buildings removed by the Japanese during the Occupation (1910-1945)—which also ended the Korean monarchy. This much I learn from bits and pieces of information on little placards in front of various buildings. The Teacher fills in the blank spots left by those brief and creatively, but not clearly, written captions. The Japanese were also responsible for the monolithic, granite modern building in front of the palace gate.

More about these places... At first, I find the palace compound to be a pretty, historical park with that strangely out-of-place square granite structure blocking it from the city, like an oversized signature or mark of censorship crossing the palace off from view. But the Teacher tells me that there has been much debate about whether to remove the insult of the occupation building or continue to make use of it as the National Museum. It is too well-built to destroy lightly, and is not unattractive as modern buildings go, but it serves as a constant reminder of the occupation of Korea by Japan until the end of World War II. Geomancy says that it interferes with the flux of positive energy in the city, blocking Korean prosperity. The current solution is a huge traditional Korean gate erected in front of the granite construction.

The antique and arts market, Insadong, is a whole neighborhood just around the corner from Kyongbok

Palace. Ignoring the incessant February rain, we meander over and eat our soup and dumpling lunch in the outskirts of this magical place before we continue to explore.

Every shop is a bit of traditional Korea. The Teacher explains to me that all the paintbrushes are for calligraphy, the huge ones being used for banners such as the ones hung throughout the city for public announcements. or like one I see on a footbridge across the road which translates to "Let's all work together for national prosperity!" I like the community spirit, and wish we had more like that back home. Other banners written with these huge brushes hang on the university campus buildings we passed on the way to the subway, and are covered with slogans for demonstrations.

The Insa-dong merchants are delighted with our curiosity. The Teacher is discovering new things, too. One shopkeeper explains the calligraphy sets, comprised of a carved stone slab, two carved paperweights the size and shape of chopstick boxes, and a water-dropper for the ink— often in the form of a little animal. The fine brushes are for personal letters or other writing. He demonstrates how a scholar holds the brush vertically, moving the hand—or whole arm—in sweeping strokes to create the letters and words. No one suggests I buy a set, which is okay. Even with this demonstration, I wouldn't know how to use it.

Many shops have a collection of stone and wooden stamps for signing official documents or paintings. I have seen people using small, wooden stamps like these for ordinary activities such as withdrawing money at the bank—apparently more secure than signing with a signature for identification, since these are all uniquely hand-carved, and signatures can so easily be forged. If you buy one, they carve your name into the end. I don't buy one today. I think about it, though. Maybe I will.

We window-shop past displays full of colored rice paper and fans; other shops are selling statuettes, including copies of ancient drinking vessels in the form of a horse and rider. My Russian professor has asked me to keep an eye out for these, so I purchase one for her. Other shops are selling green celadon jars and vases, paintings, and scrolls. Finally, we come to the more obviously Buddhist section and find wooden dinner bowls and brass bells, incense, cedar prayer beads, gray cloth for custom-made robes ... It is overwhelming, a living museum of modern traditional art and life.

At last, we catch a taxi back to the Foreign School, happy but exhausted. My parents feed us as we tell them about the day, and then the Teacher goes home. My classes at the University begin tomorrow so I get to bed early.

8

UNIVERSITY

C LASSES IN THE International Division at Yonsei University begin today, including my first classes in Korean language. I'm also taking Soviet Foreign Policy, East Asian Economies, and Korean Society and History. I am excited, and hurry through the foreign school lobby, greeting the school guards on the way through, then out the back gate of the school compound, down a stony, wooded dirt road, passing a group of students practicing with traditional drums. The road ends behind one of the ivy-covered stone academic buildings onto the Yonsei Campus.

I find my Korean class in one of the newer buildings behind one neatly labeled white door in a clean, sparse hallway with a row of many white doors. Half the other students are already in their desks—simple chairs with a small, fixed desk on the right-hand side. We are learning the letters and a few greetings, so it is slow for me and a couple of others who can already read. Even so, I expect the Korean lessons will pick up speed and then I'll be able to communicate with my new housemates in something other than impromptu sign language.

The next class of the day, Soviet Foreign Policy, is the most interesting. There are only three students enrolled: we hope the class won't be cancelled.

Our professor was a student here, he tells us, and he was quite active in the demonstrations. We are immensely curious about the inner workings of this kind of resistance, so our professor takes us for a special tour around campus. It hasn't changed much since his day, he says. He shows us where the students are preparing for demonstrations in the same way he did, brush-painting slogans on banners and preparing Molotov cocktails, stuffing a rag into the top of empty soju or beer bottles they've filled with flammable liquid, to throw at the riot police in response to their tear gas and billy-clubs.

We don't get to see all the sites of his personal political history, but he tells us how he had gotten to know the president of the college—during a sit-in protest in the president's office. He still is not sure whether that was a point for or against him when he applied for and received a scholarship to study in America, since the president was on the review committee.

Politically, it is almost as unsettled now as it was during my own first visit two years ago, when it was so serious even businessmen supported the student demonstrations by hanging long banners from office windows, and, together with blue-collar workers and housewives, they took to the streets.

After the tour, our professor takes us out to coffee. We ask him more questions. Here's how I understand the answers, combined together with what I gather from Korea History class later in the evening.

Why did so many ordinary people protest a dictatorship, risking getting arrested or even killed? The demonstrations at that time centered on an outcry against the dangerous use of tear gas, but the real cause for protest was something deeper.

When President Park Chung Hee was assassinated in 1979, people were glad he was gone. But they didn't want another military coup and dictatorship; they wanted a democracy. Democracy lasted for less than a year before another coup. Park had promised economic growth and political stability, and somewhat delivered, but at great cost. His leadership is remembered more for corruption, fraud, censorship and brutality, but also for economic growth. Was it worth it?

Park Chung Hee had arrested or removed anyone who opposed him. He instated martial law so he could shut down parliament and rebuild it with people loyal to himself, appointed by himself rather than elected by the people. He rewrote the Constitution so that he could remain president for life. Anyone could be arrested without notice or cause or a fair trial.

The next Dictator, Chun Doo Hwan—came into power in yet another coup—promising something better, but he offered no relief, instead continuing more of the same, and worse. He also intended to be president for life. One of his first moves was a brutal response to citizen demonstrations against dictatorship in the city of Kwangju. Thousands of people may have been killed, but the government insisted it was a few hundred. Instead of fearful silence, the response was outrage and more protests. Having already experienced this oppression and martial law, people were so tired of living in fear and the unpredictable actions of the dictatorship that they were willing to take the chance of being arrested, or worse.

They protested losing their freedoms, the injustice, unfair labor laws. They protested the favors given to friends of the President and those who had money and influence. The rich people could pay the courts to let them go, but the common people were punished. The common people had to serve in the army, but the rich paid their way out. The burdens of the country were born by the common and the poor, while the wealthy were given more favors and flourished. That is what we, as young Americans, barely understood.

Chun finally made some concession, promised he would only remain in office for seven years. When that seven years arrived in 1987, however, he changed his mind, using the upcoming Olympics as his excuse to remain president. He proclaimed that a turnover in government would be too upsetting just before the Games. So, the people rose up again.

Nationwide protests demanded that proper elections be held. President Chun conceded at last, but named the former general of his coup, Roh Tae Woo, as his party's preferred candidate. Two dissidents known as "The Two Kims" (Kim Dae Jung and Kim Young Sam) had both announced their candidacy as leaders of their own parties (as did a minor candidate, Kim Jong Pil). This heralded one of the first major steps in Korean democracy. Unfortunately, the opposition vote was fairly evenly divided between the Two Kims. Roh become president, but without a mandate: winning with about 37% of the vote against the split opposition.

Koreans accepted the election results and banded together in national solidarity to host the 1988 Seoul Olympics, which rolled out smoothly. Afterwards the students continued leading protests, with popular support, to assure there would be no repeat of the dictatorships that Koreans had endured for decades. The student preparation for demonstrations makes this clear.

Maybe next class we'll study Soviet policy, but no complaints here. The first day of classes, and wow, we have learned so much more than we expected.

My schedule now includes 19 hours of class, mostly mixed days of 10am-12pm, 4-6pm, and 7-9pm. Tutoring and errands in between, homework at night.

KOREA TIMES   MARCH 1, 1989

"Minjung" ["common people"] revolutionary ideology... will sweep all campuses... [It] has been rapidly spreading on campuses during freshman orientation.

9

HUMBLED

B ECAUSE THE FEW OF US in Korean class who can
already read Hangul still feel the class is too slow, we
ask our teacher to move us into the upper-level beginners'
language class. Our sweet, young teacher regards us
seriously, and agrees to let us try. We quickly decide that she
allowed us to move mainly to intimidate us, the easiest way
to teach us humility. We realize we are not ready to be
conjugating verbs and answering in Korean already, and we
only last two days in that class before returning to our
previous one. Humbled.

At last I receive word on the boarding house. The
Artist has moved, and the room is ready for me to move into
the temple tomorrow—unless it continues to rain. I don't
want anything to be drenched or dropped in slippery mud
along the unpaved pathways. The parking lot is quite a
distance from the house.

10

RAIN

NO MOVING TODAY.
When Korean skies let loose, it is all at once, and it has been raining steadily again today since dawn. An umbrella is for the optimist. I get drenched heading to classes and again later, on my way to meet my student for tutoring. My shoes are covered in mud. I rinse them off in a puddle before I enter the academic building. I'm not the only one dripping puddles of water.

Tomorrow, if it doesn't rain, I will really move into the temple.

It won't rain tomorrow.

11

NEW HOME

IT DIDN'T RAIN.

Moved in.

It is such a busy day that I can hardly stay awake to write or remember anything.

Everything I have fits into the small school van, including my bookshelf, mattress, and desk. We park in the parking lot and carry them along the paths between houses to our side temple. No one stops to ask where we were going. Everyone probably already knows. News travels quickly in little communities like this, and although I've heard there are others in homes in the main temple, I'm the only foreigner I've seen here since I arrived. The other students are out, so I move in quietly and my dad leaves. After he is gone, The Auntie of the house calls me over to meet with her.

She seems stern at first, and intimidating. She manages the boarders, who all call her *Ajumoni* (Korean for Auntie).

36

Her approval will make life here much easier, so I try to please her. I bring a basket of fruit as a gift—with bananas—an unnecessary extravagance, apparently, since they cost over a dollar apiece. She leads me to the common room where several other women, all dressed in vibrantly colored blouses and baggy floral pants, scoot aside to seat me among them. These other *ajumoni*, *halmoni* ("grandmothers") and assorted sisters, wives, and laywomen of the temple scrutinize me with great interest, and ask a barrage of questions but I can only shake my head in apology: I don't understand. They laugh and ask anyway. They appreciate the fruit. I can understand that they are interested in my hair, however, as they reach out to touch it. My shyness seems to convince them that I am a "good girl."

I pay my first month's rent: 160,000 *won*. About $200.

12

RICE PAPER

THE DAY AT THE TEMPLE begins at 4:30 in the morning, when a chanter rouses the monks to start their day. After a couple of days here I know I can open one eye, smile to myself that I have three more hours to sleep, and roll over again until breakfast is called.

When I finally must wake up, the morning sun filters through the rice paper windows of my room. The sound of birdsong and people moving about fills the air outside. This is such a different world from my parents' apartment across the mountain. A set of sliding paper doors are the entire wall at one end of my room, while the opposite end is a wall made of cement except for the rice paper windows. The length of the room is about two sleeping mats long and one wide. I have followed my housemates' example and hung a blanket across my door to help keep in the heat. I sleep on a *yo*, or futon mattress, laid out on the floor. If I stand in the middle of the room, I can touch both walls, floor, and ceiling at once with my two hands and two feet.

The floor of my room is *ondol*, meaning a floor heated by water-filled pipes. The floor was traditionally stone, but is usually cement in modern times; traditionally covered in a thick layer of golden, lacquered paper, but linoleum these days. The cement holds the heat from the pipes in winter, and keeps the room cool in summer. A wooden bench above a stone step runs around the courtyard in front of our rooms, making a convenient place to sit when the weather gets warmer. In front of each room, under this step, is a little oven where a coal brick is placed in the room's individual furnace, warming the pipes that run under the floor.

My desk is low, about sixteen inches high, so I sit on the floor when I study. Most students prefer now to study at higher desks, and some of my housemates even have squeezed high, narrow, western-style beds into their tiny rooms. I guess it's more modern. Thirteen Korean students, two women and eleven men, live in two sides side of this house. The head monk, his wife, and those of his children who are not away studying in other cities live in the other side, separated by the kitchen in the corner, and there is a small courtyard with a garden in the center. The fourth side is the bath, the flat roof covered with kimchi pots, next to the flight of stairs up to the Yongam Temple.

My door, which secures with only with a little hook and eye latch as a lock, slides open onto this courtyard. Sitting on the step in front of my doorway to put on my shoes, I am opposite those stairs, with a perfect view of the temple. The main gate is on my right, but when I go to class, I turn left from my room and take the back door to the mountain path, passing between the kitchen and the monk's side of the house.

13

BUSY

FOR LUNCH BETWEEN CLASSES today, I ask around, and join my classmate and new friend Sunna in locating one of the cafeterias on campus. We collect rice, soup, and side dishes in metal bowls on a tray, and sit at communal tables like at any other campus cafeteria. We have just enough time left to eat and rush to the next class.

When classes are over, I head up the path at the back of campus and then left to the Foreign School gate. I am tutoring a young boy after school, the son of a professor who knows my parents. She hopes for him to get ahead in English. I have two other requests, one from a woman who wants to do language exchange, and another parent who wants general tutoring for her children.

After tutoring, I make a quick visit to my parents' apartment to pick up more blankets. My room is very small, but cozy. It will be more cozy if I can figure out how to ask about the problem with the heat, or lack thereof. I've been freezing at night and bundle myself up well, including hat and scarf, with a blanket over my knees to keep warm as I sit and study during the day.

Just before dark I make my way back to the boarding house, over the shortcut on the mountain between the school, temple, and university—there is a wall, and the blankets I'm carrying make it awkward to climb over. I arrive home exhausted. My housemates notice the blankets and I find my chance to ask for help, somehow explain that I've been too cold. We can only communicate using gestures and expressions since I still can't speak Korean, but somehow we manage. I point to my bedding under the window in the far end of my tiny room, and mimic shivering. They tell me to put my bedding near the door where the floor is warmer, above the coal oven.

14

LIVING

M ORE ABOUT the boarding house.
Even after only a couple of days it is clear that living in a Korean home has different implications from living in a western style home. The traditional Korean house (like this one) consists of a series of rooms built around a central courtyard, including bedrooms, a kitchen, a common room, toilet facilities out back, and a heavy wooden double-door house gate which leads to the small street on the temple grounds. Each room has its own door opening onto the courtyard, some of them wooden doors with doorknobs, and some of them sliding lattice doors covered on one side with rice paper—all of this is within an exterior compound wall. A couple of rooms face outward toward the wall, but most of the house activity happens in the courtyard.

The roof of the house is shingled with rounded, tiles similar to a Spanish style, but black and with a rising eave at each corner, giving the impression that the house is ready for flight. The end tiles are embossed with flower patterns in a design that has some significance; I think they come from what used to be a family or village seal.

The kitchen is outfitted with a table and chairs, but the room is open and not heated. In these winter months we sit on the floor at low tables in a small adjoining room where the floor is warmed from underneath by the pipes filled with hot water. Cooking in winter must be miserably cold in the kitchen. Maybe the traditional stoves once provided enough heat, but the gas stoves don't heat the room. I feel for Ajumoni, and understand why she joins us as soon as she is done serving.

Our two toilets are out back, against the house wall. One is a urinal, the other is a ceramic hole in the floor, with a pull-chain from a tank near the ceiling for flushing. I hear that the flush toilet is an improvement on the plain hole of two years ago. It's a bit ... fragrant ... because the Korean sewer system does not handle paper well and there is a wastebasket for used toilet paper—which can be toilet tissue, magazine pages (best when not glossy), old daily calendars ... I keep tissues in my pockets.

Since the temple complex has its own gates and guard, our personal home gate is usually left open. I thought that the gate was never closed, which would mean essentially no curfew, but found that Ajumoni or one of the monks shuts the gate when the last of the household goes to bed. I don't think it is locked but it is very squeaky. Everyone would be able to hear it open at night.

15

BREAKFAST

AT ABOUT EIGHT O'CLOCK this morning, as usual (give or take an hour) Ajumoni's middle-school daughter calls us to breakfast. I have no idea what most of the dishes are, but they are delicious. The kimchi I recognize—cabbage pickled with garlic and hot peppers and it is, of course, spicy. I can't understand most of what is said.

And the chopsticks. I've been using chopsticks since I was five years old, but Korean chopsticks are different. They are slippery to hold because they are made of metal, shorter, more slender, and heavier than any I've used before. Half the food gets to my mouth, at least, and the chopsticks never quite fall all the way to the floor—well, only once on the first day, and dramatically, as I grabbed a big, slippery chunk of apple from a fruit salad. I didn't get it squarely, the chopsticks slipped in my hand, the apple flipped, and—the chopstick didn't just fall, it flew clear out

44

of my hand and nearly all the way to the next table. My new housemates gasped as they watched it fly and almost laughed but managed to be polite and hold back. Kind of. I sat shocked for a moment, then laughed for them and they joined in. What a way to break the ice. Thank goodness no one offered me a fork, only a clean set of chopsticks.

16

DINING

A T DINNERTIME, THE SMELL of food leads us once again to the several small, low lacquered wood tables in the room to the side of the kitchen. These are all set with plates of various vegetables, eggs, fish, and some dishes I don't recognize. We each take a small, covered bowl of rice, a long-handled spoon and the thin metal chopsticks, a bowl of soup, and sit down cross-legged to eat at one table or the other. All the other dishes are family-style, and we take small pieces with our chopsticks, bringing them to our own bowl of rice. The soup sits to the right of the rice, serving as beverage and soup. We use the spoons mostly for the rice and the soup.

Even though I am still not sure what we are eating, it hardly matters. Dinner is delicious. Anyway, I might starve if I were too inquisitive. What is on the table is what there is, so I can't let my particular cultural squeamishness keep me from being able to eat. I am waiting until I get accustomed to the dishes before I ask what they are made of. Mom has told me that if I don't recognize it, it's "mushrooms". There's a good chance they are mushrooms, as Buddhists tend to be vegetarian.

MJ and I eat at the smallest table. She tells me in Korean about the food, asks what we eat for breakfast and other meals in my home country, and encourages me to try some of everything. In trying to explain about American breakfasts, I learn the words for eggs, mushrooms, and bread. The concept of French toast or waffles is beyond our communication abilities for now, but "orange juice" is the same word in Korean or English.

At first, I wonder whether the tables are segregated, because we women are sitting at one table, the men at another. I remember that even at my school in the States people tend to sit with whoever is most like themselves.

After breakfast, MJ and I remain in the dining room to talk with Ajumoni, just the three of us. MJ has never practiced her English with a real live American before meeting me, but is pressed to be our interpreter. With her help, Ajumoni asks me more detailed questions than the day before. How many brothers and sisters do I have? (it's complicated, but seven), why am I not living with my parents? (to study, I tell her). What am I studying? (International Relations). Why am I in Korea? (Study, family, etc). Ajumoni has a problem trying to figure out my name, so MJ translates it into the Korean name "SuJeong," or "Crystal." Ajumoni is visibly more comfortable knowing I have a "real" name. She likes it, too, because I am very "clear," like a crystal. She is satisfied with the conversation, smiles and pats my hand, excusing us.

MJ invites me to her room for *yuja cha*, or marmalade tea. Unlike American students, my housemates always serve tea or coffee or a snack of some kind when someone drops into their room to chat or visit.

After today's classes I pick up a hot-pot for boiling water and get a store of cookies, crackers, and instant coffee packages ready for guests. I may be learning to be hospitable.

17

RUSSIAN STUDIES

I HOPE TO CONTINUE practicing Russian while I am here. I don't want to lose more than two years of study while I learn Korean. The library aid at the Foreign School writes a note in Korean explaining that I am looking for a class or a study circle. I take that note and show it to the students at the temple, hoping they can help me.

After some inquiries, my housemate MJ brings me to her older brother, who tells me about *Wekukko Daehakkyo*, or Foreign Language University, across town. He gives me directions so I can go there to see whether they will let me take a class.

I leave home at 9:30am, walk through the sleepy morning streets to the subway, and at least two hours and two hectic transfers later, I finally get to the university. The subways are so crowded--there is more life bustling underground than there is above. While it is a twenty-minute walk to the subway station nearest our house; the language university is only about five minutes from its nearest stop.

Once I locate the right end of campus, it is a challenging search to find the Russian office—Vietnamese, Turkish, Malay, then finally the Russian/Slavic Languages Department in an old, institutional building with cracking paint and featureless corridors, doors marked with old name plaques and "in/out/coming back" notice wheels which I can't quite decipher. The Russian professor is either in, out, or coming back. Whichever it is, I can hear voices and laughter coming from inside. Nervous, I muster up my best Russian grammar, knock, and enter the office.

As I pause on the threshold, the students—all men—greet me with the welcome I deserve for popping my blond head into a room, unexpected and unannounced: they all freeze, eyes open wide and stammers of "uh, um ..."

I know the feeling of anxiety, trying to come up with intelligent phrases in a foreign language on the spot. This time I am prepared for it, but the guys disrupted from sitting and joking around the professor's coffee table are caught off guard. I can see them suddenly trying to remember all the English they've ever learned, or in this case, Russian, as I introduce myself.

I realize they must think I am Russian. Even though this is a Russian department, there are no diplomatic relations between Korea and the Soviet Union. I don't know if there are even any Russians in Korea aside from an occasional official or professor who is working to create those diplomatic relations. The professor himself obviously isn't here, and none of us are making any sense to each other. We are all speaking Russian, but I don't understand their accents, and they don't understand mine. Finally, in desperation, one of them asks, "Do you speak English?" I nod, and we all breathe a sigh of relief.

It has taken until lunchtime for me to reach the university and find the correct department. The timing offers a good opportunity for breaking the ice: they invite me to join them at a local eatery for lunch.

The small restaurant is filled with students. It's a simple place with big windows, simple tables and chairs, without decoration. The menu is a series of wooden strips on the wall marked with items and prices. My new acquaintances ask me what I like. I remember the hot soup with dumplings I had with the Teacher and find it among the choices. *Mandu-guk. Mandu* is the dumplings, *guk* means soup. The word *guk, spelled the same in Korean but with a different Chinese character,* also means country, as in *Han-guk,* or Korea.

We all finally relax enough to hold a sensible conversation. It turns out there is probably no way for me to attend a course, but two of them, both Mr. Kim, are willing to establish a study group with me.

Instead of the metro, they walk me to the bus stop and on the way show me the coffee shop where we should meet next week. Symphony Cafe, it's called. There are almost no street names or numbers marked on shops in Seoul, so I hope I can find it again.

Now, nerves calmed and new friends in the making, I'm on the bus which they say will take me back to near my home more directly than the subway. More directly, that is, if there aren't any political demonstrations today or police closing off routes through the city. The students are pushing this military-connected government for political reforms just as young Korean scholars have for the past hundreds of years. Political Checks and Balances, Confucian style—respect authority, but hold it accountable, too

I make it home without running into an actual demonstration, though it takes a really long time since we have to make a couple of detours around security blockades and pass through a few fading spots of tear gas. I am lucky to get a seat at last, but is cold and now my feet are icy from sitting still too long.

The bus drops me off at the bottom of the hill on the city side of our wooded mountain. I pause to take a deep breath before I head up the steep street between smog-stained white brick apartments toward the temple. At the top of the street I pass the sign announcing Bongweon-sa, the main temple, where I nod a greeting to the uniformed guard in his small glass kiosk. From there I head through the parking lot, along the small poured concrete roadways between stone house walls topped by dark curved tiles, and turn left along a narrower pathway to Yongam-sa. The walk heats me up, and now I'm sweaty instead of frozen.

Once at our temple and boarding house compound, I pass through the courtyard to my room. I drop my bookbag on the step outside my door, sit to take off my shoes, nod hello to my housemates going back to their rooms after dinner—which I've missed again—put my shoes under the step, open the rice paper door, toss in my backpack, crawl in, and pull the door closed behind me. I unroll my bed and drop on top of it. Only for a moment. My sweat dries and I feel chilled again. I grab my toothbrush and head to the bathing room to wash and brush my teeth. The water is icy cold, but it feels better not to be covered in dry sweat. I wonder, once again, how everyone else washes. The water is so cold.

I put my toothbrush back in my room and head to the toilet outside the back gate behind the kitchen. I bring my own tissue so I don't have to use a scratchy old page from the calendar on the wall above the toilet. When I get back to my room, I change into pajamas and crawl between the quilts, exhausted.

18

BATHING

IT IS SOMEWHAT STRANGE for one grown person to have to ask another how to wash, so I haven't gotten around to asking anyone for instructions. Unfortunately, the other two women in our house are planning to move soon. If only they could stay until we knew each other better and I could ask these kinds of questions, or we could go to the public baths together. Or if only I could speak Korean well enough to ask Ajumoni—or anyone at all—what to do.

I can take showers at my parents' apartment if I walk over the ridge of the small mountain that separates us, but I need to be able to wash at my own place. It's a bit much to walk over a mountain just for a shower.

I've managed to wash my hair in a basin here, but I have to ask Ajumoni to heat some water for me on the stove. I'd do it myself, but it's her kitchen. In the washroom, I can mix the small pot of hot water in a bowl with cold water from the tank—which is really a large bathtub. I lean over a second bowl I've placed on a low stool, so it catches the soapy water as I wash my hair. It takes me forever, and my back is hurting from leaning over the basin, but at least I can have clean hair. There must be a better way, and I wish I could ask someone how to do this right.

Where does everyone else wash? We can wash ourselves with a washcloth, but no bath or shower. The water in our washroom comes from the mountain spring, almost freezing cold, and I don't see anyone else heating water, yet no one is dirty or unkempt.

I finally manage to ask MJ, and she tells me to go to a *mogyoktang*, or bath house, which includes showers and saunas. There is a good one—nothing fancy, but clean and cheap, in the neighborhood below the temple. I should look for the sign on a big chimney: a semi-circle topped by three wavy lines, like steam rising from a bowl.

19

MISSING

THIS MORNING I have to go down into the Shinchon road in front of the university before class, to the bookbinder to pick up my textbooks. We only have one original textbook for the whole class, so we take it to the bookbinder to make copies. I see that the subway entrances are lined with police checking student ID cards and inspecting book bags for political pamphlets or demonstration (the students shorten this long foreign word to "*demo*") materials. The police are trying to restrict students of other campuses from getting to our university for the demo expected this afternoon. They are also looking for certain activist student leaders. Every now and then, they arrest someone who doesn't have an ID, or who just looks like someone to pick up.

In my morning rush I forgot my ID. As a foreigner, I am not usually asked for it. If I were to be, and I spoke to them in English, they would wave me on. This saves both me and the police some embarrassment: the young police are too unsure to try to speak to me, and there are so many other people passing by that their attention is quickly and easily taken off me. I feel relieved, but also a bit guilty for that. So far I have not been stopped. Sometimes I am thankful to be in a place where English is not well spoken.

I go directly to my class, and am happy to head home directly afterwards as I can see the demo already in full swing down at the main gate below. I hear chants against government oppression and for workers' rights. In spite of the police efforts—or probably because of them—the huge demo grows violent, with students and police fighting. I hear the police shooting rounds of tear-gas in loud, popping bursts, punctuated by the Molotov cocktail bottles crashing and exploding on the pavement ... The air is already burning with the chemical dust and fire. I'm glad my classes are all at the top of campus, not near the gate. The chanting against American involvement in Korean domestic affairs, though not usually directed at individuals, makes me glad to have the back road over the mountain as my way to the boarding house, too.

I make it home, exchange brief, greetings with my housemates, then immediately go to my room to change my clothes, leaving my coat outside so that I don't bring in any more peppery powder. I grab some fresh clothes and change in the bathing room, tying my outside clothes in a bag for laundering later. I try to get my homework done.

After dinner about eight of us gather in the common room to discuss ... the demonstration? Current events? My Korean is not good enough to be sure of the details, but I know it is connected to what happened today. Not all of us are present and I know something is wrong. Ajumoni comes in with the telephone, visibly upset, and I sit back out of the way, not sure what is happening. The police have called. Or maybe she called the police. It is all rather confusing, and I don't want to interrupt to ask someone to clarify right now.

It turns out at least one of our housemates is missing. They may have been stopped at the ID check or involved in the demonstration. Many of my housemates are politically active, and one or more were likely arrested today. Another student is spending a lot of time making calls about them. I'm not even sure exactly which students are missing, or how many, as several of them are not home right now. The demo today was over labor rights, the students adding their support to the workers' cause. I hope they just couldn't get through campus to come home, but we don't know.

20

HOME SAFE

OUR MISSING HOUSEMATE came home just before dinner today. There was no laughter around the table. He silently ate with us, then went back to his room. He looks exhausted and miserable. We all feel terrible, but relieved he is back.

21

MONKS

THE HEAD MONK of Yongam-sa, the small temple where we live, is welcoming yet he exudes a feeling of solid authority, his cleanly shaven head shining above the gray cloth and dark beads of his monk's habit, not unlike the statue of the Buddha in the temple. He was very formal, but kind when I first came by, expressing an understated, polite concern that the facilities might not be what I am accustomed to. I thought of my cramped bunk in the busy salon of the ship last semester and replied that I could learn to become accustomed to them. Today he seems more comfortable with me here, acknowledging my quiet bow of greeting with the barest dignified nod as he steps out of the rice paper door of his living room, slips into his traditional white *hanbok* shoes as he slides the door closed in a single graceful motion, and passes out the gate to attend to errands.

The monks are the living tapestry of the temple. We have, in residence, "Living National Treasure number fifty": the number one Buddhist chanter in Korea. He is a wonderful old man, a quiet yet delightful presence.

When initially introduced, I bowed and said hello in Korean, "*Anyong hasimnikka?*" He simply looked intently at me, as if he were seeing into me and examining my character, then smiled suddenly, said "Hello" in English. Satisfied, he turned and went on his way. Now when we cross paths on the temple grounds, he smiles at me as if the sun has just come out from behind a cloud, and I am in a good mood for the rest of the day.

The beauty and welcome of this temple, these encounters with the monks, help me survive the frenetic activity and political unrest of the city.

This evening, I invite Sunna to come study together with me at the boarding house. We don't get much done, as the Student Monk invites us over for juice and crackers. We sit and look at photo albums of his career as a soldier while he ignores us and studies. Apparently, he got out of the military one year ago today. The uniform we see in the photos, especially the jaunty beret, shows he was in the Special Forces. We try to figure out how a monk ends up in Special Forces, but he sidesteps the question. All we find out is that he was stationed at the DMZ. And he is glad to be done with his military service.

All of my housemates have, eventually, invited me to join them and their friends for coffee or tea, which makes me feel truly welcome and part of the house. They promise to invite me to join them for movies, for coffee or go to a pub or "beer hof" on the street in front of the university.

22

SWEETS FOR THE SWEETHEARTS

THIS IS MID-MARCH, and a special holiday called "White Day," is held a month after Valentine's Day, which is red. On February 14th, the women are sweet and give chocolates to special men for Valentine's Day. A month later in March, the men are sweet in return and give chocolates for White Day. I wasn't here to give chocolates to anyone last month, but today my classmate JH gives several of us each a rose and some chocolate kisses. Then he lends me his jacket so I won't freeze walking home from class in the sudden change of weather, and another classmate invites me to join him for lunch in the cafeteria.

In the afternoon, I finally agree to meet at a studio downtown for modelling. The brand is sort of a casual sporty style: basically jeans and polos. They want blond models so their advertisements will get attention. I feel odd about it, having passed the anti-imperialism banners on my way here; at the same time I can see why they want foreigners, as I certainly do get attention everywhere I go. They have hired a couple of professional models from the States, and then us—one blond guy from the international dorm, and me. I have no idea what I'm doing, but I can't do the serious bored model look, so they get pictures of me laughing. If they like how the pictures turn out, they'll call me back about once a month.

I come home to find that my housemates have left chocolate by the door to my room, with a little note:

Sweet,
Happy White Day

MARCH 15, 1989

—

MARCH 31, 1989

23

AIR RAID DRILL

NATIONAL AIR RAID DRILL today reminds me it's the fifteenth of the month.

I can't forget that this country is only at temporary peace. The Korean War did not officially end with the cease fire in 1953, but with an armistice agreement. The peninsula is in a seemingly endless state of tension. Unification feels so far away. The demilitarized zone is closer, only twenty-five miles from Seoul, and is one of the most—if not the most—heavily guarded borders in the world. I've heard that the demarcation line along the 38th parallel can be seen from space. Every young man must take one to three years after high school and dedicate it to national security as a soldier or special police officer.

I'm on my way to meet a new English study group at a company in one of the unnumbered high-rise buildings downtown. I'm a little lost. I've heard air raid sirens before, but never when I was out in the city. And never when the threat might be real. This time when the siren wails across the city, I have just stepped out of the subway and stopped outside a video arcade, looking around for landmarks, to figure out what street I am on. At first, I think the wail is part of a game from inside the shop; perhaps someone has just won a prize. I ignore it, staring intently toward the intersection, sounding out Korean words on the street signs.

I am so focused that a man with a megaphone is almost upon me before I turn and see him, and realize he is yelling directly at me. I have no idea what he is saying, but then I notice the empty sidewalks, the quiet streets, and people gesturing frantically at me from the subway entrance. I am the only one, besides the man with the megaphone, who hasn't found cover.

All the cars are pulled to the curb, the buses have stopped, and there are no pedestrians besides the crowd under the covered subway entrance. It is a civil defense drill, and I also have to get off the sidewalk, out of sight of the sky. I run to join the people in the subway and feel safer when they pull me in and we stand squeezed tightly together as the siren wails. When the drill is over, we all pour back onto the sidewalks and go about our day. It was just a drill, but nothing to joke about. I have a surreal feeling of having fallen into a World War II movie, then back into reality. This country is still at war in spite of a ceasefire of over thirty years.

24

PUBLIC BATH

S O I'M TOO COLD TO WASH in the spring-fresh water today, and I don't want to go over the mountain to my parents' apartment for a hot shower, so I'm going to try the *mogyoktang*. I hoped MJ could go with me to show me how, but she's already heading out for a meeting with friends. I really wish I didn't have to go alone, but do I need a good, hot bath. So ... I'll go on my own and see how it works.

Through the parking lot, past the guard kiosk, down the road through the white brick houses, into the neighborhood below ... I nod to the lady in the corner store—really a walk-up the size of a closet where she sits and sells her goods. She holds up a choco-pie to entice me, but I already bought a whole box of them from her yesterday, so I laugh and shake my head no. The bathhouse is just past the dark cafe with delicious cinnamon tea where I go to study sometimes; where they let me sit for hours only ordering a cup or two. It's just before the bakery with soft sweet breads and ice cream bars in vanilla, strawberry, and red bean. I haven't been to this bathhouse, but I've seen that sign with a symbol of a bowl with three lines of steam rising up from it, so I know it's there. I'm nervous to go in, but the worst I can do is make a fool of myself, and I'm used to that, so here I go.

The lady at the desk quickly covers her surprise when I push through the doors, and greets me politely. When I pay the basic fee listed on a plaque, which I guess is the one that says *Ssauna* she gives me a key on a plastic bracelet spiraled like a telephone cord. She also hands me a thin abrasive mitten for scrubbing. I make out what must be the scrubber, *tdaesugeon* on the menu, as that has the cheapest price and the change she gives me matches the fee for the bath plus that one. It's the equivalent of a few dollars, total.

There aren't very many women here today, it seems. I don't see any men. I leave my shoes in the lobby in front of the door to the changing room next to a few other pairs. Inside I pick a spot on a bench, take off my clothes and lock them in the locker matching the number on my key, keeping the key around my wrist. It feels like any locker room from school back home, with a mustier but less pungent smell.

I watch what another woman does, pick up a small towel from the counter and follow her through the far door and into the warm, steamy bathing room. A few women are already at the showers which line the wall, not at all like the showers we wash down in after high school PE or a volleyball game. The showers are all divided by low partial walls, with the shower heads attached to hoses set in holders mounted low enough to reach while sitting on one of the brightly colored little plastic stools. Each shower is supplied with soap, shampoo, and cream rinse. I copy what everyone else is doing without actually looking directly at anyone.

Some women are scrubbing and washing their hair and then heading back to the locker room, while others are washing but not scrubbing, and heading toward one of two saunas. I pick a shower with a pink stool, put my little towel on it, sit down and set to washing too, before going into the sauna—or *ssauna*. Maybe one *ssauna* is hotter than the other, but I just choose the first one because I don't want to wander back and forth staring in and trying to decide which one. A few women are already inside, sweating. I open and close the door quickly, so the heat doesn't get out, and find a spot. We sit on our little towels on the benches and soak in the heat. Now I know why no one else in my house has a problem with the cold water for bathing. They come here.

I learned how to sauna in Finland, and it's pretty much the same here. When we are sweated enough, we go out for a quick rinse and dunk in the cold bath, then the (kind of) hot bath, then cold again, and return to the *ssauna* for another sweat. Past the baths, there are tables where we can get a professional scrubbing. One client is just finished. The scrubber sees me exiting the sauna for the last time, and gestures me over. I haven't paid the fee for the scrub, but I expect I can pay afterward, if I can figure out what "scrubbing" is called.

After the *ssauna* and pools my skin is nice and soft and ready for her to scrub. I had already showered and scrubbed off some with my little mitten in between saunas, so I expected there wouldn't be much for her to do. Clearly I had never had a professional scrub. The woman scrubs me like I've never been scrubbed before. She sloughs off layers of dead skin I could not even imagine I was carrying around, all of it falling now as a dull grey sludge onto the floor. She scrubs everywhere, rinses me and then hoses all the sludge into a side drain in the floor. It's gross and kind of embarrassing, but she follows the scrub with a light massage and I feel as fresh as a new baby.

Back at the showers I wash my hair and repeat my steps in reverse, back to the locker room, dressing, drying my hair, and putting my shoes back on. The customers' shoes have all been lined up and turned so that they are easy to step into as we exit the locker room.

I stop to pay the woman at the reception for the scrub, confusing her as I try to figure out how to describe it, finally resorting to pretending to scrub my arms. She watches me, then nods and points to *tdaemiri* on the menu, and I pay the amount. It is still under the equivalent of ten dollars. She thanks me for coming and wishes me a good day. *"Annyonghi-kahseo!"* To which I answer, *"Annyonghi-kayseo!"* The beginning of this parting greeting is the same: *annyonghi*, meaning "in peace". The second part says whether you are wishing the other person to go well or stay well. I remember this because the ending, *kahseo* means "go", and "go" in Korean is *kah*. Kay means "be", rhymes with "stay". So she says to me, essentially, "go in peace," and I respond with "stay in peace."

It wasn't really as awkward as I was afraid it would be, no one obviously too startled to see a foreigner where foreigners don't usually go. I walk home feeling fresh, and happy that the air is pretty clear from the morning rain so my new skin doesn't have to soak in the smoggy city air right away. I plan to go every weekend, if I can, making do with washcloth baths and an occasional hot shower at my parent's place when I can.

Well, I think I went pretty much unremarked at the bathhouse until ... The next day one of the monks stops and greets me—usually we nod in greeting as we pass one another on the temple grounds, or they simply pass by, preoccupied with their own thoughts or prayers. But this monk stops to greet me, so I stop to greet him and we exchange pleasantries. Then he smiles mischievously and says his wife saw me the other day, but I didn't recognize her. I wonder where we met, so I ask. "At the bathhouse!" he answers in Korean, nearly laughing. "She says you are very beautiful." I'm sure I have never turned so red with embarrassment in my entire life as I did at that moment. I can't breathe to answer. He smiles and nods, chuckling to himself, and casually walks on with his hands joined behind his back. I duck my head and hurry back to my house before anyone else can stop me.

25

MORNING PRAYER

JUST AFTER FOUR O'CLOCK, in the lessening dark of pre-dawn, the huge temple bell begins to boom, thirty times. The sound travels from the small pagoda near the main temple. It is a wooden-barred structure barely large enough to hold a sculpted, man-sized bell. A monk strikes it by swinging a length of tree trunk hung from two chains, pulling it away and letting it fall into a carved medallion on the bell. Then he catches the striker on the backswing and holds it still as the bell's reverberations linger and disappear in the distance, then he swings and strikes again ... After the fourth peal, a gong joins in, then stops, and the bell continues on. Then a single chanter. By five o'clock, as the dawn barely brightens, the monks begin to chant and beat the drum. It is six o'clock now, and all is quiet again.

26

TEAR GAS

I AM ON THE SUBWAY, taking it across town for the first meeting at Symphony Cafe with my new Russian Circle friends. Playing with current politics, I call them the "two Kims." I have to walk through a university demonstration to get to the subway, which makes me very late. I see my friends at their table in the cafe before they see me. They each have a beer and are smoking. They look up as if surprised at my arrival, as if they had a bet on whether I was going to show up and they had both bet against it. Or maybe they knew about the demonstration and hoped I was okay. Either way, they seem relieved and more relaxed once we settle down and they order a beer for me.

Mostly we just chat in our best Russian and try to learn a bit about one another. One of them has better Russian ability than I do. The other is just below me, but studies harder. They seem kind of serious, studious and a bit shy for now, but also quick to laugh and joke, and willing to meet with some strange foreign woman over beer once a week and speak Russian. They offer me a cigarette. I've never smoked, but accept it. Before I can bring it to my mouth, they both jump up and crush out theirs, so I do the same.

Their professor has walked in, and they both bow and greet him, introduce me. When the professor goes to his own table, they explain that they can't smoke in front of their professor, and women don't smoke (in public anyway), so we just give up on the cigarettes and enjoy our beer. It occurs to me to wonder why, if women don't smoke, they offered me a cigarette.

I really appreciate this friendship, because I know they are not using me to practice English, and they could hardly be interested in learning Russian from me, as my grammar is far from perfect. Until today, I hadn't realized just how often my acquaintances here are based, at least initially, on "a chance to practice English." It's nice to share a common interest.

Getting home is not difficult this time since the demonstration is over, but the sting of tear gas hangs in the air. I'm already familiar with tear gas from when I first came to Korea in 1987. Actually, it is not even a gas, but a white or yellow powder in fist-sized canisters which the police shoot from specially rigged guns, leaving splotches on the pavement after a demonstration. The bus windows rattle and the powder seeps in as we pass. We may not even see it on the street, but we are fully aware that our bus is stirring up the powder as we passengers on the bus fall into a concerted sneezing fit. It activates on our skin when it hits the moisture there—especially in our eyes—stinging, and burning in our lungs, too.

One girl on the bus doesn't have a handkerchief, so she uses her shirtsleeve to cover her face until someone gives her a spare napkin.

When I finally get home, MJ immediately recognizes what happened. She tells me to apply soap to my skin before letting water touch it, and then to direct a strong, constant stream of water from the hose in the bathing room onto my face until the stinging stops. For eyes and nose, all I can do is splash and rinse them with lots of water. As for the lungs, I'll have to wait.

Like almost everyone else, I carry a handkerchief or surgical-type facemask in my pocket at all times, ready to throw over my mouth so I can breathe a little if we hit a demonstration or its aftermath. My housemates say that mint—putting toothpaste on the cloth or chewing mint gum—helps reduce the sting. I am willing to try anything that people say will work to cut down on the way this stuff burns, so I put a few sticks of gum in my bag and smear some toothpaste onto a clean handkerchief, fold it up, and keep it in my pocket. What is this doing to our lungs?

27

AMERICA IN KOREA

AGAIN, I AM STRUCK by the incredible difference between living in Korea and living Korean. After being here at the temple only a few weeks, I have something of a shock when I join my parents at their apartment for dinner. Yes, it is easy to look at their surroundings of Korean-influenced furniture, pictures of Korea and Korean handicrafts and see that they live in Korea; but it is such a different Korea. I understand better now how it might strike a Korean as odd, or at least unfamiliar, the way Americans live.

First, the focus of the living space is up, off the floor. I haven't noticed before that there is so much space even between the floor and the table. Wasted space? Space to heat, anyway, heated with radiators in the apartment.

The couches, the coffee table higher than my scholar desk, foot stools ... things placed on the surfaces as decorations ...

The surfaces themselves ... heavy, framed pictures hanging on the walls ... a public living room connected to private bedrooms ... indoor bathrooms. Most everything is permanently fixed until one gets in the mood for the big task of rearranging.

In our boarding house, the tables we eat on and the beds we sleep on are set out for use, then put away so the floor is clear. The rooms can be smaller and multi-functional.

The modern Korean apartments are more like my parents' place, maybe, than like our traditional boarding house, but the focus and feeling here is so American—a feeling I don't get when visiting any Korean homes, except in the States. I think the heating system has a lot to do with it. With a heated floor, it is easier to orient living toward the floor to take advantage of the heat.

More could be said about the furnishing in my parent's apartment—for instance, they have a well-used oven—but I must mention the food.

A Korean meal, according to most foreigners, is *bulgogi*—literally "fire-meat" or BBQ. This is a dish that consists of marinated meat grilled at the table on a utensil that resembles a colander inverted over a small bucket of hot coals. In restaurants, the serving women bring these iron buckets to the table using only thin pieces of paper tissue as hot pads to protect their fingers—while the coals are so hot that the diners have to sit back away from them until the meat pan is placed on top, blocking some of the heat.

Served with the meat are lettuce, kimchi, red pepper and fermented bean pastes, radish, garlic, various wild, pickled vegetables, rice if you ask for it, and bottles of OB beer. I have not eaten *bulgogi* with Korean friends or in our boarding house, although people do eat *bulgogi* or *kalbi* (another marinated, grilled meat dish) in specialized restaurants or for social occasions. Maybe meat is too expensive for students—and it occurs to me that the temple is Buddhist, and Buddhists tend to be vegetarian. Whatever the reason, in the boarding house I have the chance to try many different kinds of foods—many different soups, *myon* (noodle) dishes, pickled vegetables and *panchon* (side dishes)— besides what foreigners usually eat, but not meat. Occasionally fish.

As far as I can tell, there is no Korean food designated specifically for breakfast, lunch, or dinner. Eggs, potatoes, spinach, mushrooms, many kinds and preparations of vegetables, fish, and whatever else—may be served at any time of day. At each meal, there are a variety of these dishes. We use our chopsticks to pick up the food, usually served in bite-sized pieces on a series of small dishes, and eat them with (or just before or after) a bite of rice. Usually no one takes the last piece unless there is more of the dish already prepared or unless most everyone has already left the table.

The long-handled spoon is for soup and rice. I love Korean spoons. They are an elegant perfection of spoon design. We can eat the rice straight, dip a spoonful of rice into the broth, or put our rice directly into our own soup bowls. The soup we drink during the meal; water comes afterwards.

28

DRIED SQUID

COMING HOME IN THE DARK well after midnight, I sneak up to the gate of our sleeping house and hold my breath. I've been told students, especially women, are supposed to get home early, even though no one has given us a specific curfew. In any case, our creaking house gate should be enough to make us come home before anyone is asleep. The heavy wooden door, set in the stone of the compound wall, creaks loud enough to wake up the whole house if you open it too fast. I wonder if our head monk leaves it unoiled just to keep us conscious of the hour. I push open the big red door with its brightly painted triple swirl as little as I can, slip through, and cringe. Even half a creak is too loud. I carefully push it closed with another half creak.

I've stayed out late in one of the popular beer hofs on the busy road in front of campus, studying and finishing homework with Sunna and two other classmates. The window sign announces beer and chicken. Everyone else in the beer hof was talking and laughing loudly, drinking beer and eating fried chicken. We were drinking beer and eating fried chicken too—dipping it in a little saucer of salt and pepper—amidst all the noise—but we did get our homework done, too. Nobody could be that studious, right? I figure my possibly respectable image is gone. It's late. I smell like smoke, beer, and fried chicken.

As I sneak through the courtyard MJ's brother steps out of his room. He sees me creeping toward my door and I freeze. But then I hear laughter and music—the Eagles—is pouring out of the door he has just opened. How did I not hear it? Maybe because his door is a real wooden one, not rice paper like mine, and the walls are thick. He looks at me curiously, then smiles and asks where I've been until so late.

As I struggle to explain, Ajumoni comes up behind me. She glances at us but says nothing as she passes by on her way to MJ's room on the other side of the entrance, carrying a tray holding three bottles of beer and a plate of dried salted squid. MJ opens the door for Ajumoni, sees me, and waves at me to come in, scooping her hand toward her, downward, not upward like in America—more like how we would signal someone to go away, but lower. Her new roommate is peeking around her to see who has come home and she also waves me in. I drop my bookbag in my room and join them. Then the guys smell the beer and come over with some snacks to add—my favorite sweet sesame biscuits. We finish off the beer. When they leave, I count five empty bottles instead of just the three we had to start with. Miracles. Now it is about 1:30 am, and beginning to quiet down. I had thought to be a scandal, but instead came home just as things got going.

29

WAKE UP CALL

IN THE MORNING, Ajumoni's daughter wakes us up much earlier than any of us want. At my door, she sweetly calls to me, "*Unnee, popmogo* ("older sister, time to eat rice,") and opens my door to say good morning. Then she marches to the room of the guys next to me, bangs on the door and then opens up when they don't answer, storms in and pounds on them until they swear to get up. Then she demurely goes to the next door where an older PhD candidate is staying, and because he is the most dignified of us, she respectfully calls him to breakfast without opening the door. Her etiquette is impeccable. The guys next to me always have trouble waking up when she's not around to help them.

She is growing more comfortable with me these days. After breakfast she asks me to teach her a few English words and she teaches me some Korean phrases. We eat cookies, and I show her my photos. She always calls me *unnee*, though I heard her whisper "Barbie" to her friend one day as they passed by my room.

30

SPICY

AGAIN, THIS MORNING we have a red soup with bean sprouts innocently floating in the almost clear broth. I take a sip to wet my palate for the meal—and just about spontaneously combust. Even a bite of plain rice doesn't help. The fruit salad in front of me is providential. A few pieces of pear and apple, and I can breathe again, no one the wiser. Perhaps. At least no one is obviously watching. After this, spicy food will never seem so hot again. Hah.

At lunch, we have another of what I call a red meal: kimchi soup and kimchi fried rice. As a side dish: kimchi. The water pot is mysteriously missing. My whole face turns bright red as if I have been crying for hours. Every time I have an extraordinarily spicy meal, I imagine I will become inured to the heat and it will never be able to bother me again. Until next time. My pocketful of tissues helps with my tears and runny nose.

The guys are eating with gusto, but finally, MJ notices my face, decides I have persevered long enough, and tells me I can stop eating if I want. I think I can finish my food, given a few bowls of water and another half hour or so, but we drink water from our rice bowls after eating, so there's a slight catch there. Anyway, nobody is looking for the water pot, and I have to meet my friend Sunna right after lunch...but then I look up and see Ajumoni watching with one eyebrow raised, and suddenly I can eat it all.

31

POKER

TONIGHT, MY HOUSEMATES teach me the Korean version of poker, called Go-Stop, or *hwatu*, which translates as "flower fighting." The deck has 48 small cards, with twelve suits of four cards each—I think it's for months and seasons. The cards are about half the size of a standard American poker card, and stiff. There are no numbers on them, just nature scenes with leaves, flowers, and animals. I have no idea what I'm doing, but it's really fun because, like so much about Korea, the game is very dynamic.

When you put your winning card down, you don't set it down calmly. No, you lift it high in a big circular motion and - "whack!" - toss it down on top of the others and call out "go" or "stop." I don't know what combinations constitute a win, or why we say "go" or "stop," or why this traditional game uses English, but it's fun. And since I don't know which combination of flowers or leaves or animals constitutes a win, MJ's roommate—who sits squished shoulder to shoulder with me in the tiny, crowded room—sometimes can't contain herself and points out which card I should play. When she does that, I'm pretty sure it's a win, so I call out "go" or "stop." No idea which one I should say, but I get points for enthusiasm.

My new Poker Partner is a staunch Christian and has a personal policy not to gamble or even learn to play poker for fun—though she clearly seems to have picked it up. I have a personal policy not to lose my money gambling, so she and I pair up as a great team: she gives me money, and I gamble. The profits will go to ice cream, she says. A woman after my own heart.

After a long run of *hwatu*, I offer to get American cowboy poker cards from my room. My housemates disagree with my rules, or maybe they are just lost in translation, so we play a modified version of American poker. As with the *hwatu*, none of our bets are more than 100won, or the equivalent of about ten cents or so. Before the night is through, however, MJ, my Poker Partner, and I plan an ice cream sundae party for later this week with our winnings.

32

TEMPLE HOME

TODAY THE HOUSE is already humming with activity before dawn. Later, our breakfast is accompanied by the sound of chanting and drums coming from our own temple building. It grows quiet as we finish breakfast and return to our rooms. A family descends the stairs and is led to the main room for a meal—a place the students aren't invited to go. A funeral service. They are all dressed in white mourning clothes, the men wearing black armbands, the women with red eyes and puffy faces from crying. Later I go up to the temple and see there is a new portrait draped with black ribbon, displayed by the altar. It must be the relative of that family. I leave my shoes on the step in front of one of the side doors, bow and enter into the cool, dark space. I say a prayer for him, too.

33

CLEAN ENOUGH

IN A TRADITIONAL KOREAN ROOM we sit on the floor, so that floor should be kept very clean. I just wiped my floor clean but already it feels dusty again. One could eat off of a well-kept floor. Not mine. I try to keep it free of dust and debris but find that I don't have time to wipe it down more than once, sometimes twice, a week. I guess I'm neglecting hygiene. Fortunately, the guys I live with are not too uptight themselves, so my room is neat and clean in comparison.

I seem to be constantly picking rice from my clothing. How does it get there? Messy eating, I guess. My housemates joke that I'm saving a snack for later, mimicking as if they are picking an imaginary piece of rice off their shirt and popping it into their mouths. I feel like a barbarian.

34

HAPPY EASTER

THE GUYS ARE OVER to my room this evening, and packed wall to wall. A picture party, we call it. It starts at eight, when two of the guys come over to chat, and we plan to end before it becomes an actual party so that we can all study. But we keep talking; then I take out family photos, and studies are totally forgotten.

I didn't think of the fact that American family photos are, of course, as unusual here as a foreign face—and much more interesting. Pretty soon another guy stops by, then another, and another—and we have a party. Soon all my housemates are here.

At last, I am really hosting. For the first four people I fix my specialty: cocoa coffee, but I only have four cups. Fortunately, when more arrive, they see the shortage and bring more cups and some barley cola, and MJ arrives with a bag of sweet popcorn. She combs my hair and ties it up for me.

I've borrowed some of my parents' photo albums, and I pass them around, answering questions, which come in short phrases of mixed English and Korean, gestures and pointing to the photos. We compare cultures, opinions, life in general and how it is similar or not in our two countries ... We talk of language, laugh at each other trying to pronounce hard words in the others' language. They make sure I can pronounce the city "Kyongju" properly in two syllables, and Taekwondo with "tay" instead of "tie." I help them try to pronounce "crystal" in two syllables instead of three, and "world," which is a difficult word for just about anyone who isn't a native speaker of English—and even I'm not sure if that word has two syllables or one.

They ask about daily routines in my hometown, and I ask about theirs. It's pretty much the same, getting ready for school, spending time with family or friends on weekends. I show them the books I'm reading—except for the Communist Manifesto, which is well hidden at the bottom of my trunk. On my little shelf is one historical romance amidst the sci-fi, Russian epics, a dictionary and a couple of books about Korea, a photo book of Oregon. They look at the cover, then at me, and pass it around. We laugh some more about words.

They ask about my college, and compare it to their local women's college, Ewha. I am pleased to declare our sisterhood between colleges. We look at a world map. I show them where Oregon is and brag about it as the most beautiful place in the world. They ask me about other states, such as New York and Washington (vs. Washington DC, which is just confusing), and the Grand Canyon—which is not a state, of course, but more famous than any of them. They ask about parties in the U.S. and I'm a little embarrassed to admit I don't go to many, but they are more approving than surprised.

They ask why my parents are in Korea, and I explain that they are teachers, or at least my mom is. They always wanted to travel, but their salaries were not big enough for a lot of travel. Living abroad is how they can afford to see the world. Maybe the best way to see the world is like this, living abroad.

They ask about student boarding houses in the States and I explain that we live in dorms or get our own housing in student apartments. I don't know of any Buddhist temples in the U.S., though I know we have some. I explain there are a lot of churches where I come from, in Oregon, but without the huge neon crosses that light up the cityscape in Seoul at night. We talk and talk until eleven, or midnight, before we say good night. They all help me pick up the debris from the gathering before they go back to their rooms.

I crawl into bed to the sound of someone replacing the coal in the little oven under my doorstep, so my floor will stay warm through the night. What a great place to live. I'm so happy to have these housemates. My room is covered in crumbs from all the socializing, but cozier than ever. Fifty square feet, maybe sixty, and there were about twelve people here. I fall asleep with a smile.

35

ANTI-U.S.

THERE IS A BIG anti-U.S. demo about to start at the main university gate. I have to get through that gate today to go to my tutoring lessons after classes. I hope I can make it before the demo starts.

I haven't heard from any of my student friends what the demo is about, specifically, this time. From my best understanding of the banners hanging on buildings and fences around campus, some say "Yankee, Go Home," in Korean. Other banners refer to George Bush and imperialism, and still others mention Kwangju. I believe these stem from America's acceptance of and assistance to Korean dictators. U.S. interests are interwoven with Korean domestic policy to the point that many students complain that Korea has been taken over with a puppet government of the U.S.

We continue to learn more about Korean politics in our classes and discussions with other students. When the dictator Chun Doo Hwan came into power, he continued the authoritarian style of his predecessors: he took over the intelligence agencies, installed ruthlessly violent "white skull squads" throughout the country, and sent people to "re-education" camps. This has been at the root of many protests, with grave concern over the nearly uncontested election of Chun's accomplice, current president Roh Tae Woo.

What happens under a dictator? It's still hard for me, as an American, to grasp, but we are learning. The response to the 1980 Kwangju Uprising is the kind of action we can barely imagine. The government sent armed troops against a civilians protesting against martial law, police violence, and torture for fabricated crimes—much of which has continued, even this year.

When the people of Kwangju gathered to protest, the government cut off all civilian communications to the city and then sent in tanks and paratroopers dropped from helicopters, armed with clubs, knives, and guns, all of which they used on the citizens, killing perhaps thousands. Of course, the actions of the government against its own people is still fresh in everyone's memory, and the repercussions of them are as yet unresolved.

Another reason for the protests against the U.S. is that after the Korean War, America is blamed for using Korea as a source of cheap labor and imports. The current American policy that forces Korea to open its own doors to more imports when Korea feels poor already compared to the wealthier nations of the world (like the U.S). is a sore reminder of the past and enough to keep things uncomfortably tense now.

America, with its strong influence on Korean government, did not directly intervene in Kwangju, even though they knew about it and could have. Our government still has not expressly denounced the oppression and violence, on the grounds of not interfering. The selectivity of our intervention, and its connection to U.S. interests, does not go unnoticed. We have been a positive force in Korea, but also a negative one.

When I get home, I hear of the response to the South Korean minister who went to North Korea and met with Kim Il Sung about reunification: an increase in arrests of dissidents and now even bookstore owners are being arrested, their books confiscated.

Politics, Colonization, Independence, War, Resistance, Martial Law and Oppression are recent here, real and visceral.

36

PAJAMAS

TONIGHT IN THE MEETING ROOM, where the phone is, there are seven people playing cards. It is fairly late when a call comes in for me, and for once I have already gone to bed. So I answer the phone in my pajamas. When the card players see me they are startled: "oh!" "ooh!" "hwa!" "hwaa!" My state of (un)dress interrupts the whole game. My pajamas are very modest (a sweat suit), so I'm not sure what all the fuss is about. Maybe because they've never seen me in pajamas before. Maybe because I've never been in pajamas so early before.

They think the call is from a mystery boyfriend, and they want details. They are disappointed to learn the call is from my father, who hasn't heard from me since the demonstration yesterday, and wants to make sure I am okay.

37

BULGOGI

A JUMONI IS ESPECIALLY PLEASED with me now because I ate so much lunch today. She thinks I eat too little, and is convinced that my paleness is due to being underfed. Now, for dinner she surprises us by serving bulgogi. The beef is delicious. We all sit around a huge bowl fresh off the stove, and dig into it with our chopsticks and boarding house manners. Mmmm ... bulgogi, sauces, kimchi, vegetables, lettuce, rice, everything.

To eat bulgogi gracefully takes some practice. You lay a whole leaf of lettuce in one palm and stack it with meat, a dab of *tuenjang* (pungent bean paste), *mu* (radish), garlic, and a little rice or any other flavors you like. Then, closing your hand to fold the lettuce around the meat and toppings, you wrap it up into a tight package, and plop the whole thing into your mouth ... and chew and chew and chew and enjoy all the flavors that touch every single taste bud in your mouth all at once.

Usually, we are fairly quiet while eating. This is the first time we really play at a meal, laughing with and at one another, and rudely grabbing food out from under each other's chopsticks if they are too slow—a contest of speed and skill. It is a great time and a great meal. I wonder what manners I must be picking up, living with a bunch of guys in a boarding house, but at least I know for sure how to drop the manners I have!

APRIL 1, 1989

—

APRIL 14, 1989

38

ROMEO AND JULIET

TONIGHT, THE TEACHER INVITES my father and me to dinner. By the time we are done it is getting dark, so the Teacher walks with me back over the hill to the temple, probably causing a small scandal, my showing up with a male escort after dark. The alternative is showing up alone after dark, as I do anyway, so either way they don't know what to do with me. I am just in time to meet some of the guys in my house for a prearranged session of English conversation practice that I've forgotten about. They ignore the studies and want to know more about "my friend." I feel like they are my big brothers watching out for me.

Afterward, two other guys from my house invite me to sit with them and chat, exchanging Korean and English with tea and music. Relaxing, but ... as I return later to my room, the two women in the house, MJ and my Poker Partner, come by to ask me to help them practice for the following day's English exam on *Romeo and Juliet*. We exercise our dramatic skills, which turns out to be a whole new idea for them as a method of studying. I think they enjoy it and will remember more than they would have otherwise.

They missed out on the photos at my party the other day, so before they leave we look through my photo albums, and of course the photo book of Oregon. They agree that my home state is the most beautiful place in the world—besides Korea, of course. Now I have only an ounce of energy left to write, then must go to bed, and wake up at six tomorrow. It is one a.m. now.

39

GOING THROUGH CUSTOMS

AMONG THE FIRST CUSTOMS ONE learns in Korea is to pass objects with two hands. I've heard that nearby countries have a similar custom, such as China and Mongolia, but I haven't been there, so I don't know if the custom is as strong as it is in Korea. Politeness is so essential here that one would imagine we never learn any manners in our home countries.

So much of the etiquette we take for granted in the U.S. is obsolete once we encounter this completely different kind of etiquette: How we eat; passing by in front of or behind people—pass behind a person sitting or standing; touching or not touching—you can hold hands with a same-sex friend, but not the opposite in public; who pays at a restaurant; when to speak and when to listen ... all are slightly different between here and the U.S. Myself, when I have no idea as to what details of etiquette to follow—e.g.

how to bow and when, what language forms to use, how to properly care for guest, I fall back on being as obvious as I can that I want to be polite. Being so visibly a foreigner can be an advantage: I am allowed a little extra grace, and not expected to know all the Korean rules.

Sometimes I feel badly for the Korean Americans. Here they are expected to know all the rules perfectly. But if they didn't grow up in a Korean neighborhood they may not have had much chance to practice Korean etiquette. Being bicultural has a lot of advantages, but can be difficult, too. I wish people here were more supportive of their effort.

As for passing objects with two hands ... if one is passing something important or passing to someone senior to oneself, one should hold the object gently in both hands. A variation is to pass with the right hand, holding the left hand at the elbow of the right arm. Money is a common example of the difference between Korea and America. You would never see someone toss money down on a counter when paying in a shop here, for example, like we may do in the U.S. Hand it to the vendor, politely. Regardless of the object or who is passing it, at least the right hand should be used.

Pouring drinks follows the same guidelines of using both or at least the right hand, with the other hand close to the elbow, adding that one pours for others. Don't pour your own alcohol, at least. When someone pours for you, hold your glass in your right hand, or at least touch it.

A younger person or host should be attentive to keeping a senior's glass full, and a woman is not expected to pour alcohol for a man unless she is a hostess or wife. Face away from elders when drinking, especially alcohol they have poured for you.

40

BEAUTIFUL

EARLY IN THE MORNING, I am sitting outside my room to enjoy the sunshine when a monk's wife sits down beside me and begins to chat. About something. She thinks I'm cute, and says I'm *chakha*, a "good girl." She touches my hair as she talks, maybe suggesting I get a perm, like she has, and talking, I suppose, about the best kind to get or how it would look. She is interested in my pierced ears, and the earrings I sometimes wear. She is considering getting her own pierced, but is worried about how it will feel and look. Or maybe whether it is appropriate. Pierced ears are not very popular in Korea, maybe even a little risqué.

My housemates, too, are intrigued by my foreign looks. When we are sitting together in the evenings, on the stone ledge that runs along the rooms on one side of the courtyard, the guys examine me as they discuss European (American) faces and appearance, which they decide are generally not too attractive. However, now that they are used to me, I am kind of pretty. Thanks. I think.

I can't generalize about opinions, though. Some of my other friends insist that high-bridged noses and light eyes are gorgeous--just as foreign models are good for advertisement because, "foreigners are more colorful". A foreign face attracts attention, at least, in a fairly homogeneous East Asian setting. That one I can vouch for personally. After the modelling job, I can now see myself on posters in some of the fashion shop windows. The brand I modelled for is similar to one in America that uses an "international" array of models, so I guess we do the same thing.

My housemates think I'm famous now, and congratulate me, but some people don't like the idea of using westerners to model for Korean goods which are produced, sold, and used in Korea by Koreans. It makes me think of the little blond dolls they sell for Korean girls, making them think I have doll's hair.

Today as I cross the courtyard to go out, one of the guys looks at me and spontaneously sighs, "Today is beautiful, but you, you shine more brightly." I am embarrassed and flattered at the same time.

41

CUSTOM EXCHANGE

M Y NEW ENGLISH conversation group meets today: six friends of the PhD Candidate—seven male graduate students, all about four years older than me. We meet in a cafe, in a comfortable booth around a round table. The cafes are a nice blend of large tables for groups and small tables for study. Sometimes I come to a cafe and write or study for hours, ordering a cup of tea or two. My favorite tea is *sujonggwa*: cinnamon and ginger tea with dried persimmon and jujube, so I order that. They order a few snacks, too.

For starters, we discuss what kind of introductory questions are polite to ask. The first question in Korea after "How do you like Korea?" (often phrased, "How about Korea?") is usually, "How old are you?" and "Are you married?" Sometimes I've even been asked, "How much do you weigh?" Although I don't think that question is generally considered polite here, either.

Koreans tend to be blatantly straightforward. They have heard that foreigners don't like those questions, and that Americans are particularly unhappy with personal questions about money. They want to know what they can ask when meeting a foreigner.

We decide that "hometown" questions and "Curriculum Vitae" questions are usually safe. But the awkward questions don't bother me anymore, so I tell them they can ask me anything; if the question is inappropriate or makes me uncomfortable, I'll tell them so, then maybe answer it or not.

They start out tamely enough, wanting to know about my education, and about university life in America. Of course, they also find out how old I am, and how much I weigh and that I'm not married. Then they want to know the truth concerning American attitudes about sex—as if one conversation can explain all the varying attitudes. But their only experience with social life in the States has been what they see in American movies—a version which exists mostly in Hollywood fantasies, and results in a lot of uncomfortable situations for American women abroad.

A woman here once told me she was having second thoughts about going to study in Iowa because she didn't feel she could go to parties, having noticed in movies that it was an obligation, or at least customary, to go home with someone that night for sexual intercourse. I tell them that although that could possibly happen, it is much more common in movies than in actual life, and going home with a stranger is neither usual nor an obligation. Nor advised. "Does it ever happen in Korea?" I ask back and receive no answer.

So many stereotypes, and I'm the first person they've been able to personally ask: Why do families have so many cars, why do we leave hometowns to go to colleges far away, why are Americans so obsessed with sex, why don't we respect our parents and teachers, how come Korean Americans can't speak Korean perfectly ... and it goes on.

Americans have similar stereotypes, so they ask what I mean. I reciprocate with pretty much the same questions they asked me. Why are Korean families scrambling to buy cars when the public transit is so good, why are so many students in Seoul living in boarding houses instead of at home, why are there so many cheap hotels around the university, how do Korean or American kids show their love for their parents, why can't Koreans speak English perfectly after eight to ten years of study? We are all genuinely curious about the answers.

42

MOUNTAIN WORLD

THE WALK OVER the mountain is my buffer between life here at the temple and the frenetic city.

From the side gate of our house at Yongam Temple, there is a view of the hillside, and a path that leads to a small stream at the base of the hill. I step onto the stones scattered across the water, each time hoping that a slipping rock will not turn under my foot as my weight settles onto it. I weave along a stony, narrow footpath which cuts from the stream to the main path over the ridge of the hill, and onto a steep ledge which is covered with brambles clambering down its side, rendering it nearly invisible. This then leads onto the dirt road which curves up along the low edge of the ridge.

The trees are sparsely scattered here, with a low carpet of undergrowth between them. One or two large trees grow in the road itself. Higher up, the way levels out from the steep incline, wanders past a badminton court, then past the medicinal waters of a fresh spring, a few early morning exercisers, and up to a military wall which is the real symbol of separation between this fairy green haven and the cement and smokiness of the city.

The serenity continues a bit longer, with more trees and bushes just beyond the wall, but the barbed wire on either side of the gap through which I climb is a serious reminder of a less peaceful world. I am thankful to the old uncles on the mountain, for it is they who clear the passage after the police try to block it up; a bit of civilian resistance by these men who were once themselves soldiers fighting for their country in the Korean War.

After dropping down onto the packed dirt on the far side of the wall, there are a few last minutes of the cool anonymity of green bushes and silence, and I walk down to the main road with the leaves softly brushing me on either side.

If I'm going to the university, I can continue along the path to a road to the appropriate hall, and slip into a chair in time for the beginning of class. If headed toward my parents' house at Seoul Foreign School, I cross the road onto another path, and when no one is watching, turn suddenly behind a small pine tree onto a hidden path which leads to the missionary and school compounds. Entering the Foreign School campus is an abrupt change, even with the mountain as buffer: a passage from one time and world into another ... from the chanting of monks and ancient Korean rooflines into a small Middle America and the school bell.

43

HOMESICK

READING LETTERS FROM my friends back at Mount Holyoke, I forget where I am. Today a letter arrives and I read it while walking across Yonsei campus. My friend describes our campus back home, with its spring blossoms, new construction ... and in my mind's eye I see those paths, gardens and women from all over the country and the world, at least half half of then with fair hair pulled back in pony tails, wearing sweats and blue jeans, carrying armloads of books, headed to class or studying on the grass ... what a shock to look up and not see Mount Holyoke women's college. My eyes have to refocus from what I expected to see, to what is actually here—a co-ed city campus, and everyone Korean.

Other times I get so used to the many Korean faces that I expect to see black hair and brown eyes looking back at me from my own mirror. I feel colorless. I wonder what other people see when they look at my sharp, pale features and hair among the crowd of more familiar faces. Foreign is hardly a strong enough description.

44

SPRING MOUNTAIN

S PRING FLOWERS have turned the temple, mountain, and campus into white, pink, and yellow in cavorting waves of color. Magnolia, acacia blossoms, azalea— beautifully called *chindalle* in Korea—*gaenari*, or forsythia, and even some tulips planted on campus, as well as lotus in the ponds at the temple ... Flowers line the walkways on campus and nearly cover the mountain trails. Yet soon they will all be gone, are even now starting to fall, a few blossoms wafting gently to the ground, bright petals almost like a first snow.

The main tree on the mountain is the acacia, a favorite tree for reforestation after the devastation of the Korean War laid all the hillsides bare.

It seems the whole population of Seoul is here with cameras to capture portraits with the beauty before it falls into summer heat. Maybe Mount Holyoke is also this beautiful now? It doesn't seem possible that anywhere else could be as beautiful, but our campus back home is full of flowers this time of year, too. I feel a bit homesick for my college. I've been away so long now, so many other places: Vermont, Finland and central Europe, Woods Hole, at sea in the Caribbean... almost a year away, and will be in Korea for another half year.

Beekeepers have set up their hives in the badminton court to take advantage of the tree blossoms, so the mountain buzzes, and the air is filled with bees too preoccupied to be bothered by the people who pass by.

There is a little stone shrine to one side of the spring, and I stop to express my appreciation to the mountain for sharing all this beauty.

45

RIOTS, RICE, & ROOMMATES

M J'S BROTHER TELLS ME that there will be 10,500 riot police surrounding the Yonsei Campus area today.

I'm sure I'll see them, as I have a busy day ahead: three classes, two jobs, a phone call to the States, a visit with friends, and another big demonstration happening.

Walking home at lunchtime I take the street instead of the mountain. I don't want to be alone there with so many police swarming around. But along the street I pass line after line of riot police blocking off the side access to the Yonsei campus. Almost no one else is on the road, so hundreds of pairs of eyes beneath motionless black helmets follow me as I pass. I feel afraid, so exposed and vulnerable, but I look straight ahead as if I don't see them and walk briskly.

On approaching the circle rotary at the bottom of the hill leading to the temple, I see several armored police buses; the streets are still, silent, and nearly empty but for the police.

Any sound is isolated, like an embarrassed cough amidst the tension. Suddenly, a man in a phone booth kicks the glass: it shatters with a crash that echoes around the whole scene. For a second even I am frozen. Then a few policemen take a broken step forward, stop. Even they cannot break into this space of timelessness. A dog's bark echoes like it is coming from the bottom of a well. Then, suddenly, after the pause, activity and noise return. I feel as if I have been an observer in a time lapse no one else has noticed. I continue on home to the temple; my own motion pretending it's a normal day—or nearly normal.

Later, as I return to campus for my economics class, I am stopped by the police for the first time. The demonstration is at its height near the main gate. They let me talk my way into the back of campus for my class, though I almost wish they would turn me back to the safety of home, exhausted as I am, to take a nap.

Some other foreign students are absent, including JH who never misses class. It must be bad at the main gate for him not to have made it.

46

ARREST

H IS BACK IN CLASS, visibly drained. It turns out he got arrested as he came out of the subway near the university yesterday. He is Korean-American but was afraid to even try to tell the police. Just before him a student who opened his mouth to say something got punched for the effort. At the police station the other students helped him to fill out the forms. Luckily, when the officials realized—several hours later—that they had caught an American, they let him go. He was humiliated and exhausted and so frightened: unable to understand what was going on, and afraid of what the police could do.

This is not just something we hear about; it is happening to our friends and could happen to any of us. Even a blond foreigner like me can be in the wrong place at the wrong time. I think of the Manifesto stupidly in my handbag as I entered the country ... but I worry more for my classmates, like Sunna and JH.

The White Skull Squads will go into the crowds and beat students who are demonstrating for justice or democracy. It's almost ironic that the government suppression only proves the need for demonstrations, emphasizes the injustice, making the students and citizens fight harder for democratic freedoms.

Even if you aren't speaking out, just being in the vicinity is enough cause to be arrested. Sometimes, the police don't even need a reason except to fill some made-up quota to show they are still fighting the communists, the main excuse for their authoritarianism. I have not heard of a single confirmed communist infiltrator or instigator being arrested, and that would have made the headlines, for sure. From what I can tell, most people just fervently wish above all that there could be some way to unify the Koreas: preferably under a democracy. So many families were divided.

I worry about my classmates and my housemates, more than for myself. Small consolation, but along with domestic government oppression, the foreign Empire they are protesting is the one which supposedly protects me. I feel very small.

KOREA TIMES   APRIL 14, 1989

Over 10,000 riot policemen yesterday sealed off Kimpo International Airport in Seoul and prevented dissidents and students from staging a rally to welcome the Rev. Moon Ik-hwan home... police detained some 1,200 people, but most of them were released. Thousands of students in 19 universities across the nation held campus rallies supporting Moon's controversial trip to North Korea.

118

47

GOOD-BYES

M Y POKER PARTNER moved out today. I'll miss her. Now it's only two female boarders again, MJ and I, and twelve guys at our house.

Also, MJ's brother is leaving for a few days. He sits down on the stone ledge in front of my room to put his good shoes on, explaining that he is going home for the anniversary ceremony of his father's death. His father died three years ago. Even though his father had just died, MJ's brother still had to go into military service. At least his term was shortened to one-third of the normal tour because he is an only son with no father. As such he is considered the sole supporter of his family, even though he is a student and his mother runs a small business.

I feel strange that I do not know about my Poker Partner leaving, until she is gone, or about MJ's brother going home until he is already on his way. I would have liked to have prepared a goodbye gift or card.

48

WHITE PETALS

TODAY I GO into the side temple to the Mountain Spirit and sit with the old Man and the Tiger for a while. I thank them for sharing their beautiful mountain with me.

The walk over the mountain is so fragrant now, almost buried in the white petals fallen from the blossoms in the trees. Crossing over at night these days, the ground glows as if completely covered in snow, and in daytime the air shimmers with more petals falling, shaking in the wind and blowing along the ground.

This must be what nostalgia looks like. The mountain makes me feel this is all a dream and I'll wake up back in my dorm room at Mount Holyoke, with the memories of this world fading away.

Old Man and the Tiger smile at me as if we share this secret, but only they will remember.

49

HALMONIS

M Y "TWO KIMS" AND I meet to study Russian. Last week we met near my university, and this week we meet at theirs. On the hour-plus bus ride to get there, I mostly read in my seat, then stand up for an elderly woman who gets onto the bus at a later stop. She pulls the bookbag from my hands and holds it on her lap. When the seat in front of her becomes free half an hour later, a young man who has just gotten on sits down. She makes him move for me. He moves, of course, we bow a little to one another, and I sit down.

The *halmoni* pats me on the shoulder and I turn to her. We fall into an easy camaraderie—smiling, laughing, and trying to talk, even though we don't share a language, and will probably never run into each other again. She points at me, and then at a family on the bus. With gestures, I explain my parents, my siblings, and holding up my textbook and pen case, show her that I am a student.

The Korean *halmonis* (grandmothers) are so free and beautiful. Everyone answers to and respects them. Once she celebrates her sixtieth birthday, the Teacher explained to me, a Korean woman finally has approached the top of the social hierarchy. Of course she is never the patriarch, but he said that they no longer have to worry so much about staying properly in their womanly place. Perhaps, after sixty years, they finally decide they've been at the bottom long enough, and all the strength they've been gathering throughout the years comes out in new power and freedom.

I see *halmonis* at the temple singing or dancing and chatting with friends, taking advantage of holidays and beautiful weather to meet and have a good time, and maybe enjoy a bit of rice wine. They are also known for insuring that no one makes things difficult for them. With their strong elbows, they always end up first in a bus line...and they are known for their great sense of humor and bright, ready smiles, so expressive even a non-Korean speaker can understand them.

50

ADOPTED

AT THE END OF BREAKFAST, the Student Monk plops a huge, pressed ball of rice—I think it is a monk's snack food—next to my bowl and says, "Eat, for school." The ball is a treat made from crisped rice from the bottom and edges of the pot, mixed with a little sesame, and held together by virtue of the moist rice in the middle. A great snack, and I will savor it slowly. It looks like he is taking care of me because of what happened when my parents came by the temple yesterday. I am still not sure how I feel about it.

The Student Monk was passing through the courtyard. When he saw them he began to greet them with his usual politeness, then suddenly stepped back as if stunned and looked more intently at my mother. I looked at my mother, and she was startled, too. It was like they recognized each other, like they were meeting someone they hadn't seen in a long time.

He pointed at me, then at my mother. "Mama?" he asked her. She smiled and said yes. Then she pointed at him and said, "My son." He bowed and said, "Mama." He gestured to himself, then to her, "My Mama." I'm not sure what my dad thought, but I'm pretty sure we just witnessed two people recognizing each other from a past life. I think she just gained a new son. After living here for the past couple of months, it feels as though nothing is impossible.

51

HOSPITALS

I HAVEN'T HAD A FREE MINUTE this week that someone hasn't needed me. I have barely even written anything in my journal.

The little girl I've been tutoring, just six years old, is in the hospital. Families are responsible for some basic care for a family member in the hospital, including meals. During the day, I've been in classes, lunchtime tutoring, modelling, afternoon tutoring, and helping my own mother get ready to go to the States for surgery. Nights, I have been at my little student's house taking care of her older sister so that their mom can stay at the hospital with her. I'm really worried about my student, although her mother assures me it isn't serious.

52

PEACEFUL

A N UNUSUAL DEMO TODAY.

KOREA HERALD   APRIL 14, 1989

Students and dissident figures, holding
placards, banners and pickets, shout slogans at
the main entrance of Yonsei University after
holding a rally denouncing the arrest of Rev.
Moon Ik-hwan yesterday. The demonstrators, in a
rare peaceful gesture, did not use firebombs
and rocks against tear gas-firing police.

53

PRE-DEMO

ANOTHER GREAT LESSON about demonstrations and politics this morning. My father and I pass through a pre-demo on our way downtown, hoping to get to the subway before the police block access. As we cross through the gate from Seoul Foreign School onto the forested road to Yonsei University campus, we step around students curled up, wrapped in their jackets and sleeping anywhere that they could find a slightly comfortable bit of ground. Students who weren't already there during the day had to sneak in during the night, before the police blockades had completely shut off all access routes to campus. We see students are camped all over the university grounds, now beginning to awaken and prepare for the demonstration.

The university is transformed for demonstrations every few weeks. This time, a much bigger demonstration than usual has been prepared. Our professor tells us it is the anniversary of the April Revolution of 1960, when the students and citizens rose up and eventually ousted Syngman Rhee for his authoritarian rule.

The revolution began with protests against Rhee amending the constitution to take a third term, and then exploded with the death of a student who had been apprehended by the police and then found in a reservoir. Syngman Rhee was ousted, replaced by a confusing series of presidents and parliament for less than two years, and then a military coup put Park Chung Hee in power as dictator for the next seventeen. Park is credited with great progress for Korea, but also for brutal leadership. Another short presidency, followed by another dictator, and at last, today, there is a chance these demonstrations will truly set in place a new era of democracy for Korea. It is exciting at the same time that it is frightening and dangerous.

The university today is lined with large, boldly painted banners hung from every building, and on a scaffolding that has been erected at the end of the main promenade. It is perfectly positioned to be visible even from the main gate and the railroad embankment outside the university, where the photographers of both foreign and domestic media have also camped out for the night, securing the best camera angles they can get.

The banners surrounding us are painted in almost communist style, but more colorful and dynamic than the typically muscular, industrial-looking Russian or Chinese propaganda. Many of them were likely painted in the rooms our professor showed us on the first day of Soviet Studies class, but some look too big to have ever been inside a closed space. Some of the posters are very dark and sinister, illustrating the crimes of the police, the government, or American imperialism.

More banners and photographs, slogans, and news bulletins are posted on any available space along the main promenade, representing every cause I have ever seen or heard of being defended by the students, as well as labor concerns. The photos captured by American photographers will provide cover images for the major U.S. news magazines and papers, prompting friends and relatives in the U.S. to write and ask, once again, whether we will be evacuating sometime soon. We don't plan to.

There are memorial banners of students who have been killed, banners for unification, for a new government, for communism, for democracy, for socialism, for anti-Imperialism, cries for freedom of the press and information and assembly, for the release of political prisoners, for better working conditions and better wages, for justice, for protection of the Korean market, for freer international and inter-Korean travel, for everything. Many of them are things I hardly thought about as a student in the United States. Today is promising to be the biggest demonstration I have ever seen or imagined.

Then we come closer to the main gate itself, where students are gathering an hour before the scheduled commencement of the demo, clapping and singing, wearing headbands and surgical masks or wrapping scarves around their faces to protect from tear gas powder. But the demo has not begun, and what they are singing is not the usual demo chorus. They are singing folk songs. The police are Korean too, and they cannot resist the familiar songs of love for their people, their country. They join in the singing. Then one of the policemen and a student leader join arms in the middle of the street and begin to dance together to the music. Folk dancing.

How little we understand Korea. And how insignificant we become. They can dance and sing together, those whom

131

we simply describe in our national newscasts as mortally opposed, and our only part in it is represented on anti-imperialist banners hanging down the face of the library.

We can see that the demonstrations and tear gas should start within the hour. We turn and head back up campus to the East Gate, where we hope to catch a bus or taxi heading away from the demonstration. We have errands to run to help prepare Mom for her trip back to the States.

We find out later that this was just the beginning. The demonstration isn't over, instead is growing, with more students finding their way onto campus, and more demonstrations expected tomorrow.

APRIL 15, 1989

—

APRIL 30, 1989

54

AND POLITICS

AIR RAID DRILL TODAY, but I don't have to seek cover. My student's big sister and I are both studying quietly at home as we hear the siren wail, so we stay inside. It is a Saturday. We weren't going anywhere, anyway.

Soon after, my little student and her mother come home from the hospital. She seems tired, but happy to see me, sorry to see me leave. I'm happy to see her as I've missed her, too, but it is time to take my own mother to the airport. Like turning a page in the same book, my mother is headed to the hospital, but in the States, for surgery and recuperation until sometime in May. I have been worried about my student all week, and now I switch all that worry to Mom.

As soon as I leave my student's house, I rush home to help carry Mom's bags across to the parking lot while my father goes to catch a taxi. He avoids the university, and instead heads down the hill to the smaller street in our own neighborhood where it might be easier to find a taxi. He walks right into the aftermath of the demonstrations that have grown so huge they encompass even the neighborhood in Yonhui-dong. In addition to all the main issues, they are also in response to Reverend Moon Ik Hwan's return from his trip to North Korea

Although many Koreans yearn to be a united country again, any contact with North Korea is highly controversial, and especially unsanctioned talks of re-unification make the government nervous. Some are demonstrating to welcome him and protest his arrest; others to protest his trip and support his arrest.

Dad tells us the streets below the school compound are littered with tear gas, broken stones, burn-stains and glass. He couldn't get a taxi, is just back, sneezing, and his eyes are red and burning. He dumps his clothes in the hall of the apartment because they are covered with tear gas powder and heads straight for the shower. While he showers and Mom prepares to leave, I am scrambling to get a ride or borrow a car to get us to the airport, because even the buses won't pass near this road until the debris is cleaned up.

One of the school guards offers to drive us. Taking back streets and private roads he somehow gets us to the airport just in time. My parents have always been friendly with the guards and other school support staff, and I guess that helped him decide to risk the journey. On the way out the back way, I discover that our compound is neighbor to some very elite citizens' homes.

REUTERS APRIL 15, 1989

Protesters from both right and left staged demonstrations Friday in Seoul amid increasing furor over a leading South Korean dissident's illegal visit to North Korea. Thousands of

South Korean war veterans marched through the capital demanding the execution of Moon Ik Hwan, a 71-year-old Presbyterian pastor arrested when he returned from the visit Thursday. Students and dissidents staged demonstrations on more than a dozen South Korean campuses demanding Moon's release. Police used tear gas to subdue firebomb-throwing protesters.

... Moon could face the death sentence or a long jail term if convicted of pro-communist activity under Seoul's draconian National Security Law.

55

WORRYING MY HOUSEMATES

AFTER RETURNING from the airport and doing a load of laundry because of the tear gas, once again I come home well after dark. I can hear my housemates in the next room trying to figure out how to say, properly in English, "What makes you come home so late?" I wonder what sentiment is behind the question. I know that I don't act appropriately for the ideal of a Korean woman's behavior, so I hope it is not resentment of that. I hope they just wonder what a foreigner finds to do all day.

Then I realize that of course they were worried about my safety. Between my student and my mother's hospital situations, I've been gone for over two days. I had tried to explain I'd be away taking care of my student's sister, but maybe it wasn't clear. Maybe they didn't know where I was or why I was gone. They must have worried I'd gotten caught up in that demo. None of us are really safe, and we are all worried when someone isn't home.

Aside from these past few days with my student's sister, I'm not even sure myself why it is that I don't get home until so late—often too late for dinner—except that maybe it's because I live in so many worlds: the temple, the university, Seoul Foreign School, tutoring, study circles ... demos and air raid drills, too, I guess. I give Ajumoni my parent's number, but I don't know what she can do with it. Maybe if she calls, my parents could find someone who speaks Korean to talk with her. I give her the number to the guard desk at the school, too.

56

POLITICS AND GHOSTS

THIS EVENING, we are on blackout for national security. If the armistice were to end and return to active war, we would have to be prepared for bombers, so it is our duty to make our homes invisible to them by turning out all lights or blocking windows. We sit in dim candlelight and tell ghost stories at our house to lighten the mood after a heavy discussion on politics. With all the regime change underway and the prolific number of demos, politics is a common topic. But it is a serious one: it is not theoretical, but rather active thought about what can be done to improve the country. Part of improving the country includes how to make it more prosperous and self-reliant, and that includes addressing international relations and American influence, generally referred to as imperialism.

To wash away the discomfort of the topics settled like ash in this small, dark room, and to help us leave as friends after all this talk, we change the subject. The ghost stories begin: hardly a light change of topic, but at least a change.

First, my housemates tell me, seriously, that the mountain is full of ghosts: the occupation, the war, lovers and families torn apart. It turns out that this is one of their concerns for me, crossing the mountain alone at night. I haven't felt afraid, though I haven't always felt alone on the dark path, either.

In the candlelight, my housemates roll up one guy's sweater and stuff it into another, filling it out like a body. Taking various bits of clothes, they create an eerie life-sized doll. The head they make with a towel and pinch the features of a deformed face into it. At the doll's feet they set a candle. As the flame slowly flickers, the eyes of this makeshift doll seem to blink and gaze around the room at each of us.

With the burning of the candle my companions invent a story of a girl who died here because of a bomb that fell during the war. The fire that followed horribly disfigured the child. Her father was killed as a soldier, and her mother, returning home from over the mountain with what plants she could gather to feed them, sees the house on fire and yet is unable to find her child. Then she hears her daughter crying for her and runs into the house to save her, but is unable to reach the child before dying in the flames.

Now the ghosts of mother and child are forever searching for one another, yet never meet. They say the child is now looking for anyone who will love her, yet if someone gives in to her cries, their spirit, too, will be doomed to wander in loneliness and search for love. They make the story up as they tell it, but we can feel the truth of war behind it.

57

SOCIAL SOLITUDE

E VERY DAY IT SEEMS there is someone new passing by or through our house. I never know who they are, though I presume most of them are friends of one housemate or another, or here to visit the temple or the monks. Today a man left a note in my room for "The American woman who lives here," which is now only me. But the note is not for me, and I save it for the other American woman—the Artist—who lived here before me and will be visiting in a few months. Another friend once received a letter from overseas addressed simply with "Canadian. Ron. Seoul, Korea." He received it directly to the room he rented in a home in Seoul, without much delay.

Everyone presumes the man is leaving the note for me and wants to know who he is. Of course, I have no idea. They tease and imply at first that I am being coy. I'm learning to presume that whatever I do will be noticed by someone or everyone. It must be the same for the others, too, but my housemates have heard that Americans like more time alone than others, and usually try to respect that, at least in their own way.

It is an odd combination, living here with so many other people. Someone is always about, and everyone knows everyone else's business, but there is solitude, too. This is a feeling that I hadn't experienced in America—that another person's nearby presence or noise does not necessarily feel like an invasion of privacy. I think it's related to the Korean way of recognizing not to see something that should not be seen. If you don't want others around, you just don't notice them. It's not necessarily conscious, just necessary.

58

LOVERS

MJ, THE ONLY OTHER WOMAN student in our house for now, and her big brother are both moving tomorrow to an apartment. Her brother's best friend, who has been his roommate, is pretty sad. Me, too. We'll miss them. And I'll be the only woman boarder left in the house.

I remember when I first met her brother. His roommate, who speaks a little English, introduced us saying, "This is my lover." Somehow, I doubted this was what he meant to announce to me on our first meeting.

I said, "Oh, you are friends!"

"No," he replied, "We are lovers."

Hmmm. "What do you mean?" I finally asked after we had gone in circles for a few more rounds.

"He has been my friend since childhood, and our families are very close, so we love each other like brothers. Therefore, we are lovers."

He was embarrassed to find out that "lovers", in today's English, means two people who sleep together sexually (because he and his roommate do share a room and thus "sleep together" I had to qualify that idiom, too). He was distressed to discover that there is no word to distinguish close from casual friendship, except the infrequently used word "acquaintance" or the qualification "close" friend.

59

MOUNT HOLYOKE IN KOREA

I HAVE BEEN INVITED to dinner with the Assistant Director of Admissions from Mount Holyoke, who has just come to Korea. She is visiting my parents' school, so the high school advisor is inviting me to join the two of them tonight.

I enjoy eating some home-made American food: casserole and veggies. Maybe not elegant for the American visitor, but my delight must show, and she looks at the meal differently, realizing it is special to us.

As we talk, it turns out the Assistant Director was on the admissions committee when I applied to Mount Holyoke three years ago, and she remembers my application. In particular, I am embarrassed to learn that she remembers my essay. I had already completed all my college applications when I learned of Mount Holyoke, only days before the deadline. The essay question was, I believe, on current events. I'm from Klamath Falls, Oregon, and the biggest current event in my mind was the seasonal migration of birds, stopping by our lake to feast on the fish and bugs of Klamath Lake. She remembered and appreciated it, she says, because nearly everyone else wrote about the threat of nuclear war. I wonder if she also realizes I typed that application on a turn-of-the-century Underwood typewriter, since my mom wouldn't let me touch her electric one. I don't mention it, as I'm already provincial enough as it is, compared to my urban classmates in the U.S.

They think I should write a book about living here in Korea. Strange as it may sound on paper, the past couple of months have come to seem commonplace to me now. It takes a conscious effort to pick out the unusual. I'm a student, going to school and living in a boarding house. How we eat, our rooms and the house, customs, and habits seem not much more unusual than campus life in the States.

I guess it is being immersed in a situation that makes it seem ordinary. Talking with the counselor and representative gives me a second-hand glance at how my ordinary days look from outside. I tell them I am keeping a journal and trying to pay special attention to these details.

The Admissions Director is exhilarated by the vibrant activity of Seoul. There are so many people, that every walkway and every street is crowded with movement. Coming from New England, the change from the long, pale faces predominant in Massachusetts to the round, colorful Asian faces and black hair here is quite a contrast. The architecture, the language, the wild taxis, the fragrant and colorful food, the visual chaos are all new to her. After living here for a while, we get used to it. I see Seoul anew, through her eyes.

Yet she hasn't done anything specifically "cultural," so I invite her to visit me at the temple. At least I'm not so used to living here that I can't recognize that it would be a special treat to have a personal tour of it. She says her schedule is so tight that she thinks she may not be able to fit in a visit. I'm sure she wants to say no, but we press her anyway, and she promises she will try to make time. How could she fly so far, we insist, and not see this hidden bit of Korea that so few have a chance to see? She tentatively agrees.

60

ADMIRERS, SPICE AND DEMOS

THIS AFTERNOON when I get home, there is a birthday present sitting next to my door. My birthday isn't until next week, but I won't tell. Wouldn't want to embarrass anyone, right? How nice, now, that my birthday will last an entire week!

The next morning, I am greeted by flowers outside my door... someone has taken a cue from yesterday's gift and left them as an early belated birthday present. I love flowers. And the vase is a jar decorated with a handmade ink drawing of grasses and petals. I just bought a celadon vase at a little shop for such an occasion as this, but how could a store-bought vase be more beautiful than this homemade one? My next early birthday present is that the Admissions Director has agreed to come visit this weekend!

Birthday or not, visits or not, we also have to study for midterm exams. One today, two Monday. I set the vase aside, dress quickly, and go to the kitchen for breakfast.

Breakfast is rice, spicy-hot bean-sprout soup, tofu lightly battered with a seasoned omelet, salty smoked fish, kimchi, something marinated that seems to be a fish or meat, or vegetable (mushroom?), lotus root, *kim* (roasted, salted seaweed with sesame oil), something else that looks like a vegetable, and something else. And fruit salad. Delicious. I study all morning. Just as I am ready to take a lunch break, the popping sound of tear gas canisters reaches us here. It sounds like popcorn. If the wind is strong enough, and blowing in our direction, even on the other side of the hill we feel the sting of that powder—just enough to remind us what is happening.

61

TEMPLE TOUR

I AM SO HAPPY that the Admissions Director has made time to visit the temple, joined by the Korean alumna she had an appointment with. Their amazement is more than I expected and reminds me how unusual this all might seem to someone from outside—even a Korean from a different background. Would other people from back home see it as they do? They are both so excited about every little detail, and things I don't even notice any more, that their visit makes me reflect on what "exotic" means.

What I think the Admissions Director would find boring or antiquated is instead fascinating to her because she's never seen anything like it: the guard at the main gate, monks going about their business and the sound of music coming from temple buildings...the rough poured concrete, people with light backpacks and bottles coming to the temple for spring water, others praying in the temples, the garden in our courtyard, taking shoes off at doors, the petals decorating the rice paper of my door, the dimensions of my room. Her interest is something like the curiosity my friends here have about daily life in an American dormitory and campus setting. The rules are different, the food is different, the rooms are different. I must keep all this in mind when life gets too routine; look at it through new eyes, think about how to describe even ordinary things to someone who has never seen them.

Almost as interesting as the Director's reaction is that of the Korean alumna who brought her here. She comes from a completely different background, lives in a modern apartment and, as a Christian, has not seen this part of her own culture either. Even the news of Korean campus life is interesting to her because she spent her college days in the States at Mount Holyoke.

The Korean alumna has to leave on schedule, but the American admissions representative wants to stay to see more. She takes pictures of the buildings, of our house, of the kimchi pots, the doors, and even of my room. No one has ever taken pictures of my room before.

I look at our home through her eyes, and see an exotic, cramped room that would almost fit in a doll's house. My wooden chests, brightly blanketed and folded bed, the low scholar desk and floor cushions, the rice paper window.

The Admissions Director needs to use the toilet before she leaves, and asks to see our washroom and the toilets — literally water closets. I am reminded of how tiny and dark they looked to me when I first arrived, and how strongly they smelled of damp and, well, toilet. It has taken me some time to become comfortable with the two footpads and a porcelain hole instead of a seat on a pedestal toilet. I used to hold my breath against the smell; I don't notice it much anymore. She is brave, and survives the experience.

Most visitors comment on the smells of Korea, but I think they usually mean the kimchi, which is made with garlic—a smell which pervades everything and is especially sharp in the subways and buses on hot days. Maybe an added smell of old plumbing, too.

I take her to the parking lot, where the guard stops one of the taxis dropping off a visitor. We give the taxi driver directions, and send her on her way. My heart aches with a little homesickness as I watch her taxi disappear down the hill.

62

NORMAL DAYS

TODAY IS ANOTHER GOOD but exhausting day: exam in the morning, tutoring at noon, studying and more tutoring from afternoon to evening. Then out late with friends, by chance.

Some of my housemates and I have agreed to go out to a movie, but I am too late after tutoring, so I've missed our meeting time. As the taxi stops at the bottom of the hill, and before I can get out, three guys jump in and order it downtown. In my surprise, I don't even see who they are. The taxi driver is also shocked for a moment.

Then I realize they are my friends and I tell him it is okay. They had waited for me, but finally decided to leave—just as I arrived. Our paths crossed just in time. What a surprise.

It is great to be part of such a close-knit group and so accepted as their housemate when I am so different. I am the "junior" of the students who were here before me, the "senior" of those who move in after me (as far as the house is concerned). And I have extra respect now, especially from my (younger) "senior" in the house. Once when he was teasing me, I mock reprimanded, "little brother!" He immediately apologized and I was embarrassed at having embarrassed him, but it seems I had accidentally shown an unexpected understanding of the proper state of relationships.

Little Brother. It seems now that, apart from that one guy younger than me, that's my informal title among my housemates. In the taxi they explain why they can go with me to the movie so late ..."You are not a man ... but you are not like a woman. So you are like our little brother." Now they treat me more seriously, though we all still play and joke around. We are more comfortable with one another, and I fit in a little better. They might have told me this earlier, I think, but maybe waited until MJ was gone. I was already enough of a bad influence on the other women in the house, perhaps, without them including me as one of the guys. Whatever the reason, I enjoy being part of this house, and I am amused to be a "little brother."

63

TOO MUCH RUM

I WILL HAVE SUCH A HEADACHE tomorrow when I turn twenty-one. Sunna and other friends from Econ and Soviet Studies classes took me out for a birthday party tonight because my dad is making dinner for me tomorrow. They found a good club downtown, where we began the celebration. The waiters never ask how old we are, and I don't even know what the drinking age is in Korea. My friends bought tropical rum drinks to remind me of the sea and brought silly gifts.

There were so many of us that we couldn't all fit at the table at one time, which was fine since we'd rather be dancing anyway. The staff of the restaurant didn't like that we brought our own cake, but they let us light candles and all, just as long as we didn't eat it there. Of course, once it was on the table in front of me, well, we just couldn't leave it ... so for my birthday foolishness, aided by the hand of the friend next to me, I had to take a bite of the cake. The cake now has a nice imprint of my face on one corner. We had to put it back in the box to save for tomorrow, and it is sitting in a cold corner of my room. I had thought to bring it to my parent's place, but maybe not with the faceplant on it.

Too tired to write any more.

64

TOO MUCH SOJU

WOKE UP THIRSTY and a little groggy, but no headache. Today is my twenty-first birthday American age, but my Korean friends celebrate this as my twenty-second, Korean style. If I were Korean, I would be considered one year old at birth, having spent about that long in the womb, and then have gained a year of age every Lunar New Year rather than on my birth date.

And what a birthday! Four cakes!

The first is the cake from last night out with friends at the club, which is still sitting in my room; the second cake is from my classmates, shared during Korean language class with the iconic Korean alcohol, *soju*; the third is from my dad, who makes me a home-cooked dinner, followed by a home-baked cake; and the last is a cake my housemates pick up at the bakery at the bottom of the hill, waiting for me when I stagger home in the dark.

Dad's cake is a yellow one with chocolate frosting. I haven't had a homemade cake in a long time—nor the foods he fixes for dinner: steak and baked potatoes with real cheese, fresh spinach, salad ... He likes to fix "typical" American meals for special occasions. He must have shopped at the Black Market in Shincheon Rotary, near my usual subway stop. On Thanksgiving, he even manages to get a turkey, and he fixes the entire traditional meal, for Christmas, too. The traditional foods are even more special when they are difficult to come by. The home-baked potato is heavenly.

As for getting to that dinner at my parents' place, that is a little more difficult. My teacher and classmates insist that I get drunk for my birthday. I refuse, largely because the upcoming dinner with my dad, his boss, and her young son is scheduled just after my class gets out at 6:00. I relent just enough to let my classmates pour me a token amount of soju, not realizing how strong it is. Or that I have a lot of classmates, and they all want to pour some for me. It tastes very light; no coughing or burning sensation. Just fine until I try to move and realize my coordination is, um, not so graceful.

I try to think very sobering thoughts as JH walks me to my dad's house, and manage to be seated before Dad's boss arrives with her son. Can I behave well enough that maybe they won't notice? I hope. She wants to know all about how I enjoyed the Admission Director's visit. I smile and say it was wonderful. Fate steps in to help me: she has already followed up with the director, so she tells my father all about it, and I don't have to. I find this hilariously providential, but I keep my sense of humor well in check, even though it is ready to come out in wild laughter. I "casually" lean on the arm of the sofa most of the evening to keep the room from moving. She must have noticed.

159

When his boss leaves, I apologize to my dad for being drunk. He is surprised, says he hadn't noticed. I guess the sofa did its job holding me steady. He makes me stay for a while before he lets me head home. It's almost dark by then.

Coming into the house on the mountain trail, through the back gate, my housemates surprise me with one more cake and several bottles of beer. I have spoons in my room, so we eat the cake with those. No plates. They are happy to drink most of the beer.

65

THE WALL

THE DEMONSTRATIONS are getting even more intense. The city adjusts to the blockades, but sometimes we miss appointments, unable to get where we are going. This rebirth of democracy is exciting even while it is a little frightening. Last night the temple parking lot was filled with police buses, being the closest parking lot of any size near the university.

This morning as I head over the mountain to class, I am almost afraid to continue on. Soldiers are everywhere. They are friendly: just a bunch of young guys waiting to be called to duty, but by sheer numbers they are threatening, too. I am hoping they will not be in the clearing where I usually climb over the wall, because it will be a huge detour to get to class if I have to go all the way down the slope to the official gate, and I will be very late. As I top the ridge, there don't seem to be any more soldiers, so I decide to chance it, and turn into the hidden picnic area by the wall, heading toward the hole in the barbed wire.

There are no normal soldiers here; the picnic area is full of officers. I don't see them until I've turned the corner. I stop mid-step, and their conversations halt as they see me. Not many foreigners walk on the mountain, so I'm usually a shock even to the picnickers and people who gather water from the spring nearby.

The officers look at one another, trying to decide who has to talk to me. A young guy loses out and approaches me to ask where I am going. "Uuuhhh ..." I answer.

He looks where I am headed, and like a hound I am pointing directly to the hole in the wire, which he might not have noticed otherwise. Anyway, he seems surprised, and again asks where I am headed (besides through the hole in the wire). "To class," I tell him, intentionally using the most fumbling Korean possible. The audience of officers laughs. I show him my schoolbooks.

"Aahh," he says, and walks to the wall. He inspects it and calls me over.

The lump in my throat must be as big as my neck because I can't swallow my fear. I approach the wall, and he says something to me that I don't understand. The other officers are watching intently. They discuss something with one another and call out to him. He gestures for me to come right up close to him at the wall. He points at the wall and asks me another question. I can't understand him, and he gets frustrated, as he cannot speak English. The other officers call out to him again, teasing him.

Suddenly the young officer turns to me and pushes his radio into my hand. Dumbfounded, I stare at it, while he climbs up the wall and looks over the other side. He comes down, takes the radio back, and pulls my books out of my hands. The other officers laugh at my surprise. He takes my hand, and like a gentleman, helps me climb over the wall through the cut in the wire. Once I am over, he hands my books across to me. I thank him in my most awkward Korean. He smiles and tells me to go on, then says good-bye to me in English—which makes the other officers burst out even louder, the sound of their amusement following me as I turn the corner. As soon as I know they can't see me anymore, I run, hoping I can get away from them, and make it to the lecture in time. I hardly breathe until I am settled, shaking a little, into a desk in the auditorium.

The lecture I was headed to turns out to be well worth the difficulty of getting to it. The speaker grew up under the Japanese Occupation, and talks about the:

- Korean people's response to liberation (including dancing in the streets).

- American military's violent reaction (soldiers fearing the Korean celebration was the revolution the Japanese had "warned" them would come).

- division of the country as the Japanese colonizing power surrendered to both the U.S.—in the south, and Russia—in the north: because neither side wanted the other to have strategic control of the peninsula.

- Allied rejection of the Korean government returning from exile in China and Manchuria, putting colonial collaborators back in power because, apparently, they already knew the ropes.

- new feeling of occupation as what many considered a puppet government is installed. By the U.S.

- Korean War.

- political turmoil following.

These are still major issues inspiring the student demos today, forty to fifty years after these events.

The guest speaker also had been a captain in one of the coups, and later studied in top U.S. universities. He is an excellent speaker, and keeps us all leaning forward to hear more.

I hear that the police have left, so I return home over the mountain in the afternoon and approach the wall tentatively. The soldiers, officers, and the branch we prop against the wall to climb over are all gone, but the barbed wire has not been repaired, so I pull myself over the wall and continue back to the temple.

MAY 1, 1989

—

MAY 14, 1989

66

COUSINS

M Y COUSIN WILL BE VISITING. It is amazing that
family can find us even when we are tucked away
here in this corner of Asia. So many Americans don't know
where Korea is—I didn't know, before we moved here—but
too often presume it must be near the Philippines because
the two are usually shown in succession on CNN. And then
no one wants to visit because the killings and kidnappings in
one place get confused with the political demonstrations of
the other. I can't wait to take her to all my favorite places and
to show friends that I have relatives.

Since most expatriates are here alone, it is sometimes
assumed that our families are not very important to us. In
Korea, family connections are essential. My cousin's visit
will be a nice chance to show my friends here that our family
relationships are strong even if we are expatriates. People
are surprised to imagine that a young woman my age is here

alone, but pleasantly surprised to hear that I have family who live in Korea, too. When we are together, the aunties have fun comparing my mother and me for family resemblance. If my stepfather is with us, they usually say I look like him. My mother always protests, but Dad and I are pleased. Anyway, to have a cousin here, too, means we care about extended family.

I can't wait until she gets to see our temple. She has read about Kyongju and Jeju-do (*do* means island) and wants to go there. I've been to both before, as a tourist, but I won't be able to go with her this time. No vacation for me.

On her first day in Seoul she goes to my parent's apartment, talking over what to do and where to go. She decides to start with Jeju-do, the major island off the southern tip of the Korean peninsula. The climate there is warmer and has a different culture, an island culture centered on the sea, including real mermaids. It is wilder there, with less crowds and cement than Seoul, for sure.

We help her plan her trip, eat dinner, and at last I remember it is time for me to get home. She wants to walk with me over the mountain, knowing she will have to spend the night. I'm happy to show off our house to her.

As we pass through the back gate of the school, I decide not to take her through the chanting we can hear on the mountain—not temple music, but rather the chanting of slogans, including those against American foreign policy, in preparation for tomorrow's demonstration. We take the roads instead. Even if we were not American, as foreigners it is best not to purposely walk into shouts of "Yankee go home!" The students are on the university side of the mountain, between us and the military wall that marks the border of campus, a zone presumably safe from the police.

The long way home is a long walk around, and we are ready to sleep when we arrive. I give her my bedroll, and I sleep on a quilt on the floor next to her. In the morning, she meets the Student Monk and my other housemates over breakfast, and works hard to manage the food with the tiny metal Korean chopsticks. I translate as best I can between her and my housemates. She is wide-eyed at what sounds to her like perfect Korea, while the guys are amused with my clumsy translations. Fortunately, laughing and enjoying new acquaintances needs no translation.

I assure her she is doing fine with her chopsticks, that the only necessity is to get a piece of food from the dish to her mouth without dropping it. My housemates are aghast when they realize what I've told her. "No!" they insist, "That's wrong!" I am stunned and embarrassed. Then they continue sternly, "It doesn't matter if you drop it, as long as you can get it to your mouth." We all laugh, especially me, in relief. We continue eating. But when she drops a slippery piece of fruit onto the table, she gasps, then when she is sure we are all watching, she dramatically grabs it again with her chopsticks and fingers, slowly brings it to her mouth, and chews it up. Her mischievous curiosity and energy surprise, baffle, and delight the other students, Ajumoni, and the monks.

After brushing our teeth in the clear, fresh water piped into the bathing room, I give her a tour of the temple buildings and grounds. I show her how one ought to make half a bow before entering a temple, and only a monk in prayer robes should enter through the center door.

When we return, we have tea with the Student Monk and the housemates who hadn't woken up for breakfast. Then I notice too much time has passed, and I have to run over the mountain to class.

The guys discuss what to do with my cousin, and they decide the Student Monk can escort her home to the Foreign School gate when he leaves for his classes at his university in another part of the city. He knows the way, he says, and my parents later confirm that he has been stopping by for lunch sometimes, or bringing them small gifts and plenty of laughter. He is delighted to have found some parents. My father still seems a little perplexed, while my mother is whole-heartedly happy to have a son here in Korea.

67

DEATH AND TRUCE

THE DEMOS HAVE SLACKENED OFF a bit since a tragic event in Pusan last week. Six policemen and a student were killed by a fire in the university library. The students had apparently drenched a barricade with paint thinner, and either they set fire to it, or the police shot something that ignited it. The fire spread to the library. The government usually blames the students, and the students usually blame the police.

As a result, however, the government seems to be making moves to scale down the violent response to demonstrations, encouraging more peacefulness on the part of the protestors in turn. They say there will be no tear gas fired unless Molotov cocktails are thrown first. And the police will not prevent protest marches unless "necessary". Everyone is happy at the thought of no tear gas, but hardly optimistic that the government will adhere to the terms of its own proclamation.

68

JEJU-DO

"WATER, WIND, WOMEN, AND ROCK," are the four famous qualities of Jeju-do. The Water is the sea, And the waterfalls which drop from steep, volcanic cliffs directly into the surf. The Wind is the constant breeze, gales, and scouring winds which sweep across the island. The Women are famous for their strength and beauty, mermaids famous as deep free divers who support their families with shellfish and other sea creatures they gather from the ocean, rocks and sea floor. The Rock is the very volcano which formed the island, the cooled lava from which the houses are constructed, as are the fences, pavement, sculptures, and most of the island itself.

My cousin has returned from Jeju-do; happy, wind-blown, and a bit sunburned. Water, Wind, Women, and Rock ... And in modern times, she informs me, was one I hadn't thought of: honeymooners Jeju is also a must-go place for honeymooners to take photos for their wedding albums.

She was fascinated by the dedicated tours for the honeymooning couples. Huge buses full of newlyweds pull into the parking lot at one famous site or another, she told me. At once, all the couples get out to look, then line up to get their pictures taken in front of a certain statue or angle of the waterfalls or piece of bridge. They hand their video cameras to the bus driver—or taxi driver for private tours—so he can film them running dramatically across the beach into each other's arms. Or with the still camera, to shoot a picture of the groom seeming to stand in the bride's hands—by having him stand on a dune in the background while she holds up her cupped palms. The scenes are sweet, sincere, and fun, until the obligatory sights and scenes become exhausting, especially with brides in their high heels navigating the paths while carrying the bulk of the camera equipment and luggage while their new husbands scope out the best of the preordained sites. We wonder whether everyone has the same wedding album in the end. Maybe that's the point.

69

ROCK, PAPER, SCISSORS

T HE CHANTING OF MONKS in the temple is now mingled with the sounds of children playing *kawi, bawi, bo* (rock, paper, scissors, but actually scissors, rock, paper) on the temple steps. Today is Children's Day, May fifth: no school, no classes, children everywhere being given treats, cakes, and lots of attention. The sun is shining, and the air is fresh and warm.

The Student Monk takes me to visit his little niece, who has studied a few words of English, but does not believe anyone really uses them. On the way to his sister's house, we stop at a bakery to pick up a small but exquisite cake.

She is a beautiful child, dressed up for the day but shy in front of me, a stranger. The Student Monk takes at least a roll of photographs, a very proud uncle. The little girl is smiling and laughing at all the attention we give her, but for every photograph, she suddenly becomes serious and sedate, breaking into laughter again only after the shutter has clicked.

Back home, studying in my room. One of the children outside is using a peashooter, getting rambunctious with the holiday mood and the warming weather. A stray pea shoots a hole through the rice paper near the top of my door. I look up from my book at the loud popping sound. The pea flies clear across the room to the rice paper window on the far wall, missing me by a couple of inches. I open the door to see the child hiding behind the thin tree in the courtyard garden, but he comes out and giggles when I laugh.

70

NEW FRIEND

ONE OF THE TWO KIMS of our Russian study group brings his sister to our meeting near my university. She is an English education major, so she is interested in meeting this native speaker friend of her brother. It's a special occasion, so we go for Chinese food, which today means *tangsuyuk*, or sweet and sour pork, but nothing like the Chinese food we have in the States. I don't know what the word means exactly, but this is breaded and crispy deep-fried strips of pork (or chicken or beef) served on a platter with a bowl on the side filled with peppers and sweet onions mixed into sweet and sour sauce. And we order *Jjajang-myun*. This is hand-pulled wheat noodles, with vegetables and meat in black bean sauce on top. We mix the sauce thoroughly into the noodles with our chopsticks, then eat. *Myun* means noodles. *Jjajang* is the black bean sauce. Yum.

It hadn't occurred to me that Chinese food would be different from back home in the U.S. I guess we had an early immigration mostly from South China, while Korea is closer to north China. This is more north Chinese food. In the north, they grow wheat; in the south, they grow rice, so the northern foods tend to include more wheat products like these noodles. It's not a hard and fast rule, of course.

And every restaurant meal includes barley tea—hot barley tea is served in winter, cold in the summer. It's offered with every meal, the way we put ice water on the table in American restaurants. It's one way to know the water has been boiled. Chinese white kimchi is the side dish, as well as fresh onions to dip into a thick black bean sauce—thicker than the sauce on the noodles, and without the vegetables and meat.

Talking with Kim's little sister makes me realize just how few female friends I have. It is something I really miss after the close-knit confidences of Mount Holyoke. She is a bit shy to speak English with me, just as I am shy to speak Korean with her, but we try, and we enjoy eating noodles together. I hope we can meet again.

Amidst introductions and political discussion, the guys mention that my hair looks a little different. But only a little. I tried to get a perm yesterday, but the hairdressers are not used to my kind of hair. My hair is very thin, not very porous, so the chemicals didn't soak in and the curl didn't take. I guess. This gives Kim's sister a chance to feel my hair. It is the first time she has ever felt blond hair. Soft, like doll's hair, she says. She invites me to her school festival coming up.

We were supposed to have met the week before last, but cancelled due to the demos. Then we were supposed to have met for Russian last week, but the demos and poor communication confused things. We typically schedule our meetings at alternate universities, meeting one week near their university, the next week near mine. Last week I thought we were to meet here, they thought there. So we waited, each for two hours in our respective cafes, imagining that the others had been caught by the traffic, the tear gas, or the police. We had no way to contact each other until we went home. They called my house afterwards, and left a message with my housemates to meet here this time.

71

PREPARATIONS

B UDDHA'S BIRTHDAY IS COMING!
It is more and more difficult to get to sleep and stay
that way through the night lately. New people are passing
through our house early in the mornings and late into the
night ... maybe in preparation for the festival. The monks
are active earlier than usual with the holiday approaching.
Usually, all is quiet after the early bell and prayers until about
seven o'clock, but today the chanting has been continuous
since before sunrise.

At our house, we have begun making lanterns for the
celebrations—cutting and assembling bright paper,
snowflake-like flowers, streamers ... The festive mood is as
catching as Christmas back home.

Ajumoni is planning a special meal for tonight in the
spirit of all the work and excitement in the house. We are
all almost as excited to see what she will prepare as we are

about the growing stack of paper lanterns and paper flowers. She is gone most of the day shopping to buy the ingredients.

She is caught in the demo, and barely makes it home. When she finally arrives, we take her bags and set them in the kitchen. She tells us to handle them carefully, wipe everything down and throw away the bags. She has to bathe to get the tear gas off her skin and out of her eyes before she can even think about starting dinner. Water hardly helps, since it activates the powder, but a lot of soap and then water are better than the itching and burning on the skin and in eyes and lungs. When she has washed away the worst of the powder—it is impossible to get it all off once it has irritated your eyes and skin—she prepares an inspired feast with the special vegetables she has brought. In spite of the stress and struggle of the day, she makes us all full and happy.

After dinner, I am supposed to leave to meet my English study group, but the household will not let me go. I insist several times that I can avoid the demo by taking back routes, but they insist just as strongly that I am crazy if I want to go anywhere at all tonight. So I stay home and listen to the popcorn sound of tear gas canisters being shot off. I am glad not to be out there.

72

NEW RICE PAPER

TODAY WE GET TO RE-PAPER the doors and windows of our house before Buddha's Birthday.

First, we remove the doors and windows from our rooms, lifting them off the wooden tracks. We set them out in the courtyard, spray them down to soften the glue, and then tear the paper off the wooden latticework. Some of the paper is torn or has holes anyway, where we have punctured it accidentally or intentionally rubbed a spot with a wet finger to make discreet holes to see outside. Once most of the paper is peeled off, we spray the doors and windows with water again and scrub until all the residue is removed.

Meanwhile, Ajumoni is making glue, boiling some rice in too much water, mashing it as it cooks, then letting it cool.

When the wood is clean, we brush the rice water glue onto huge sheets of thick mulberry-fiber paper with a hand broom and carefully place the paper back against the wooden lattice. It sticks immediately and will be impossible to remove without ripping once the glue dries. Some of us pick leaves or flowers from the garden to glue onto the paper so that when light shines through, it illuminates the colored petals and leaves. Now that the doors are back up, the whole house looks refreshed.

73

MOK-TAK, WOODEN FISH

B Y DAWN IT IS RAINING a light mist.
Standing outside the kitchen on my way into
breakfast, I look up to our temple and see a gray and red-
robed monk seated inside the open central door,
chanting, his back to the opening. It is a slow prayer now,
muted by the rain, and punctuated by a low hollow beat
on the wooden *mok-tak*.

Yesterday, after we finished papering the doors, two of
the monks took me around the temple grounds. They tell me
that, since I am living here, they should make sure I
understand a little about what the temple is for. I've picked
up bits and pieces, but my lack of Korean makes it difficult to
understand details. So, yesterday they took time specifically
to explain the stories behind several paintings and
instruments that can be found in most of the buildings. We

used my dictionary to work out the stories with a mixture of Korean, English, and lots of gestures and acting.

The *mok-tak*, or wooden fish, looks like a hollow wooden ball, kind of like a bell, with a handle. It can be found in every temple building and heard almost any time, but especially at dawn and dusk. The monk taps it with a wooden striker, slowly but not too slow, fast, but not too fast. The story behind it I understand is this:

Once upon a time, so long ago (when tigers smoked long pipes, they say), there was a young novice monk who was very poorly behaved. If there was anything wrong to do, he did it. He was so terrible that he died and was reborn as a fish. This was especially dreadful because a monk should be nearing the end of the reincarnation cycle, and to be reborn as a fish is a huge drop in progress. He was not only reduced to being a fish but had to endure further pain because a tree grew out of his back.

One day his former teacher was sailing on the lake and recognized his student. Seeing what pain the tree caused the fish, the teacher took pity and pulled it from his back. When the teacher arrived home, he carved from the tree a round wooden bell that resembled a fish with its shape. Whenever this bell is struck, the sound should remind all living creatures of the bad novice's fate. All living things should pray for those poor creatures like the novice-turned-fish and remember their own behavior.

In the morning this wooden bell, or *mok-tak,* is played with a progressively louder and faster rhythm, and in the evening the sound becomes softer and slower until the evening prayer is finished.

74

POLLUTION

THE POLLUTION IS SO BAD, some days we can't even see the tall buildings in the city. On bad days, if you blow your nose, the tissue turns black. Sometimes, especially in springtime, the air is yellow when wind patterns blow dust from the Gobi Desert in Mongolia, across China and into Korea. I think that dust is part of why the Yellow River is yellow.

I wear more makeup than usual, which was usually none, because my skin is breaking out and I'm guessing it is from the pollution. It can't be good to breathe, either. A lot of people wear masks against tear gas, but also if they have a cold and don't want to cough or sneeze on other people, and because of the pollution, too.

This evening, after I've washed my face and studied in my room, my housemate next door stops by to ask whether his music (the Eagles again) is bothering me, and I tell him no. Satisfied, he goes back to his studies and his music. As I turn from sliding the door closed, my eyes catch the reflection of my face in the little mirror on my wall. Until this moment I have forgotten that there is acne cream spotted over possible offenders on my skin. He didn't even blink or smile. He didn't see what he shouldn't see? Oh well.

75

AUNTIES

RAIN IS POURING DOWN TODAY, but Ajumoni and the monks say that it will not rain tomorrow and spoil the festival. Buddha's Birthday is tomorrow! It never rains on Buddha's Birthday: the sky is just clearing the air for the holiday.

The outdoor lanterns are all made of paper, and the elephant and dragon for the procession are papier-mâché. Man-Bong Sunim, the Living National Treasure of Buddhist painting has prepared a huge backdrop of Buddha for the outdoor dancing, prayers, and speeches that should take place in the main courtyard. It can't rain tomorrow, so I guess it won't.

My mother is scheduled to arrive back in Korea tomorrow, too. She is excited about the festival, and so disappointed about missing most of it that she has insisted that I stay at the temple and take pictures instead of meeting her at the airport. I feel torn but stay as she asks.

About twenty women are here now, cleaning up the temple and decorating and hanging the colorful paper lanterns, giving directions to the monk's sons and student boarders who have offered to help. Those who have beautiful handwriting, or rather calligraphy, are writing names of sponsors on streamers to hang on the lanterns. I join them, and the Student Monk shows me that my family's names have already been written on the streamer of a lantern. He was the sponsor, and we are his family.

When we go outside for a break, the guys teach me the words for some of the features surrounding the temple: the ladder for hanging lanterns, pine trees that serve as a natural backdrop, tiles making the roof soar. In the festive mood, the monks have me try on the butterfly robes for *nabi-chum*, one of the Buddhist dances. They take my camera, and take turns to get a picture with me in the high, square hat, the wide sleeves edged with ribbons, and the robe reaching to the ground, my shy face and blond hair peek out from under the hat. They ask me to make them a copy. The aunties smile and laugh and tell me I look pretty.

MAY 12, 1989

HAPPY BIRTHDAY, BUDDHA

76

BUDDHA'S BIRTHDAY

FIVE-THIRTY IN THE MORNING, I hear the head monk of the temple waking up his wife and sons in the rooms across the courtyard, his voice a quiet rumble. He speaks only once and they are stirring with hardly a sound, soft rustles. The temple day begins in stages. We students aren't called to breakfast for another hour or so.

I stretch, try to go back to sleep, but am too excited to sleep until it is my turn to wake up. I pull on my jeans and T-shirt, fold up my bed, and cross the courtyard to the kitchen to see if I can help with preparations. None of the other students are stirring.

The family and visiting helpers—laymen and women in grey pants and jackets—are startled to see me. Some newcomers stare in surprise at the sight of me in the house, so out of place here, while others who are more used to the sight of me ask "Are you awake so early?" "Why?" "Aren't you cold?" "You should get some more sleep: it's a big day," and then, happily, "Today is the holiday!" "Your parents are coming?"

Finally, convincing me that I am more of a distraction than help, they persuade me to go back to bed. They awaken all of us an hour later for a quick breakfast of soup and rice. There are so many visitors in the house today, and the phone barely drops back onto the hook before another call comes through.

More early visitors come in at a steady pace, climbing the granite stairs to the temple above our courtyard, joining those now already bowing and praying, filling the building, one of our monks leading in chant. The familiar view of the monk in his grey and red robes is framed by the center door. Guests' shoes cover the granite steps in front of the left and right-side doors. The visitors enter the temple building where they murmur prayers and bow to the floor in front of the Buddha, stand, and bow again, three times, then kneel and pray some more until they are done. They pray for the Buddha, for their families, for health, peace, and prosperity, and wisdom: for all the things people around the world pray or hope for.

Unable to use our busy phone to arrange with family and friends when and where to meet, I walk up to the main temple to use the pay phone. I have to wait in line. I guess our phone isn't the only busy one. I give up and assume we'll find each other, easier for us because we stand out as almost the only obvious foreigners in sight.

The sky is clear, not a drop of rain. It never rains on Buddha's Birthday, so the day has dawned blue and crisp.

The usual quiet of the temple grounds is already transformed with color and commotion. Vendors are lined up in the parking lot, selling treats from carts or carrying baskets of food and trinkets among the crowds, musicians are playing pipes amidst beggars, monks, papier-mâché animals and joyful visitors laughing, dancing around people still waiting for the phone. No one could be in a bad mood today—even the beggars are happy, everyone generous and sharing. Only the monks and some laymen are preoccupied, moving with purpose, carrying trays of fruit, candles, boxes or baskets, focused on all the preparations and guests and activities.

On the way back to our side temple, I pass gray-robed monks hanging rainbow-striped paper lanterns on long wires which crisscross the main compound. Each lantern trails the paper streamer printed with names in handwritten calligraphy. My housemates and I venture out again with cameras, taking rolls of pictures like tourists in our own territory.

By noon it is impossible to walk anywhere in a straight line. Everywhere are groups of people, especially older ones, shoulder-dancing to traditional music, laughter aided by a bit of *soju* or *makkoli*, a light rice wine, happy and reaching out to bring passersby into the dance.

The paper lanterns soon form dense, luminous canopies over every open space, each now being fitted with a small, white candle to be lit at dusk. The temple is more crowded every moment —children with or without their parents nearby, more street vendors setting up, couples taking pictures, and more foreigners than I have ever seen here. My family and I cannot even find each other. Having lost track of friends and housemates as the crowd pushes me forward, I give up and am happily sitting squashed shoulder to shoulder amongst strangers when the monks' dancing begins.

One of my housemates, who is acting as photographer for our temple, finally catches sight of me and pulls me closer, in front of the crowds of spectators, to sit with him. We are pressed so far forward, we nearly touch the mats where the monks dance, turn and clap flowers or cymbals together, spinning slowly or suddenly to the music of the chanters and musicians who sit just as close on the other side.

As the sky darkens into dusk, gray-robed volunteers light the lanterns. We are glad to be just far enough forward to be out of the way of any dripping wax from the candles. Soon the lanterns form a canopy of light. Surprisingly only a couple of the paper lanterns catch fire—both just as they are lit—and are immediately pulled down so the flame does not spread. The wires gently sway, and the view of the temple must appear as a sea of rippling light from the hikers' outlook on top of the mountain behind us.

Nightfall at last. The prayers, music, dancing, and official festivities are over and the courtyard quiets down as almost all the visitors go home. A few drunken celebrators remain behind. My mother arrived at some time during the festivities, along with the rest of visiting family and friends. We find each other at last. My cousin has wax drops on her clothing; she considers them a badge of honor.

My family are invited into our house as special guests and treated to a wonderful meal, as is the custom for Buddha's Birthday, offering food to visitors. I think the meal they are offered is extra special. They are delighted with the wild vegetables, lotus root, soups, pickles, and sauces. The table blooms into a bright display of colors and mingling aromas as Ajumoni and her helpers bring in more and more ceramic bowls, tiny or large according to the dish, stacking new ones into pyramids on top of the ones they've already set before us. Every food is intentionally as beautiful as it is delicious.

Can there be a more perfect holiday? For my mother, Buddha's Birthday is certainly the perfect welcome back to Korea.

77

MOTHER'S DAY

THIS MORNING I GO OUT to Shinchon, the main street and neighborhood in front of the university, to get fresh flowers and a new Korean/English dictionary for my mother. The streets are quiet, it being an early Sunday morning after a wild Saturday night.

When I get home I run into the Student Monk, who invites me to attend a ceremony he will be dancing for in one of the temple buildings. I agree; he nods goodbye and runs up the hill to the main temple. I understand it should be about half an hour, leaving me time to head over the ridge afterwards to have lunch with Mom and wish her a happy Mother's Day. Instead, it turns out he meant the ceremony would begin in half an hour, and continue for almost three hours. I'll be missing lunch.

I'm not sure exactly which temple building to go to. An elderly monk notices me wandering around searching for the source of the music that floats across the grounds, and tells me to follow him. We approach a temple building which has just gone quiet. During the lull in the music he guides me in, points to an empty cushion where I should sit between two monks. The floor is warm. The room is crowded. Many, many whispers suddenly among the family members across the room as they see a foreigner join the ceremony.

The smell of incense is strong and heady. The monk seated to my left begins ringing a bell while the Student Monk sets a faster rhythm with a brass gong. The chanters join in. The bright tempo and the backdrop of brightly painted roof-beams and pictorial stories on the walls give the ceremony an almost dizzy sensation of an elaborate play— but the family in white mourning clothes and armbands clearly indicate this is a funeral.

We sit around the edges of the room facing the altar and a statue of a Buddha. In front of these are brass bowls filled with sand for holding incense sticks, in front of the plates of offerings in honor of the Buddha and the deceased. These offerings are in the form of fruits, bright-colored candies, or rice cakes, all layered up to almost two feet high in swirling patterns. The gray and red-robed monks are seated in front of us closer to the altar, with their chant books and musical instruments.

Several pairs of large, brass cymbals are set in a line along the floor in front of the incense bowls. The chanting goes on and on, rising and intense. In the midst of it, in one smooth motion the monks stand, as do the family members. The pace of the chanting remains unbroken. After an interval of suspense, everyone bows, and a monk begins leading the mourners in a procession circling the room. I stand uncomfortably now by my cushion, alone and unsure of whether I should follow, too, or not interfere in the ceremony—if this is just for the monks and family. One elderly woman sees my consternation and smiles, motioning me into the place just before her. We circle the room again and again, chanting and saying a rosary that I do not know.

At last, we sit down, and the chanting takes on a new tone. After a minute, the Student Monk puts down the gong he was beating and walks forward to pick up a set of cymbals. He stands, waiting, cymbals in front of his chest. A haunting windy pipe begins to play. Another monk appears from somewhere and takes another set of cymbals. The two monks stand together before the altar, facing the Buddha.

Suddenly one brings the cymbals together in a crash. Then the dancers are still again, now holding their cymbals before their faces like quivering communion platters. Then the cymbals come together, vibrating, and just touching, closer, lightly, lightly, until the sound ascends into a roar. Then, crashing cymbals together, the monks begin to dance. The dancers whirl the cymbals up and down, up, over, behind their heads. They whirl with them as they turn and play. The cymbals slide together and crash and roar and spin. Then, abruptly, they cease. The dancers wave the cymbals together into a bow and set them back in their resting places before the Buddha.

The two monks return to their pillows and again become seated chanters. Somewhere in all of this, the sound of the windy pipe music has disappeared. The chanting and drums and gongs grow so loud that when a monk begins to ring a bell, it is soundless in its motion. After the first dance, the pattern of the ceremony begins again, but in opposite order.

Chanting, dancing, procession, chanting. The Student Monk has put on new robes, transformed into a butterfly dancer, and we encircle him as we walk. The sound of the haunting pipe returns, rises above the chanting, leading the butterfly movements or being created by them. When the family rises to leave, I slip out the side door, and follow a silent way over the mountain, where the falling petals of the trees are like warm snowflakes in the shimmering air. Halfway over the mountain, I sit down amidst the swirling petals and write.

This story is Mom's Mother's Day gift.

78

CUCKOO

BIRDSONG ACCOMPANIES SUNRISE, sunset, and every walk over the mountain. One of the loudest is the cuckoo, who is just getting started, as if slowly learning to coo ... at all hours, even into the night. At first, it only cooed once or twice, then more times every day. Every day the sound is louder and bolder than the last. They say that if you count the number of coos, that will tell you how many years you will live. I plan to hold off counting until the birds have had more practice.

MAY 15, 1989

—

MAY 31, 1989

79

FORTIFIED

AIR RAID DRILL TODAY.
Korea really is a fortified nation at uneasy rest. This occurs to me for the hundredth-some time as I climb over the cement wall at the break in the barbed wire, then jump down and walk along a ledge that is the soil-covered roof of the storage room or bunker. All I can see of it is a bit of cement wall and a locked door. It is where I sit during the air raid drill today, my back to the wall, knees drawn up with my bookbag resting against my shins.

The mountain is quiet as I wait for the "all clear" siren. There are no police today and only a few water gatherers. I'm not sure why the soldiers don't care much about this place where we climb over the wall.

They clearly know about where we can climb through at the bottom of the wall, too, as that is more often patched — but a new hole always appears. And the gate down the hill on the other side, that is only sometimes locked, and is hardly very secure. I climb over it if I find it locked when I need to detour that way to avoid police. It is a little strange that there is a wall here at all, when it is possible to get to both sides of it without much trouble.

Maybe the point is just that it's there. Every hill is nominally controlled by the military, so maybe every hill needs a wall. This hill still has trenches and sandbags in an area much higher up than I usually go. They cannot close off the hill completely, though, because of the temple and the fresh water. And aside from the mountains, there are no green spaces in the city.

80

PUPPY

ALONG WITH THE EXCITEMENT of the celebrations last weekend, we now have a new puppy. The poor little guy howls all night, crying for attention and to be let into a room. He is a sturdy *Jindogae* puppy, a Korean breed of dog, *gae* from *Jin-do*, or Jin Island—golden-tan with perky ears and a curly tail, especially known for their intelligence and home-guarding abilities. They are not considered indoor animals, however.

Dogs as pets are just barely coming into fashion. They are still mostly considered either food or working animals, Jindogae falling into the latter category. There was a pre-Olympic campaign to end the food category, but it has not gone away entirely. I once saw a live animal market, where one could buy chickens or ducks—or dogs. They were all in stacked cages for display, and somehow the canines lacked the dog spirit we attribute to them in the U.S. They were just like the resigned chickens and ducks. As for our puppy, he is mostly spoiled and adored. We fuss over and play with him during the day, but at night, he cries in the courtyard when he is out there alone.

81

NATIONAL SECURITY BLACKOUT

AT HOME AFTER A LONG DAY, wafts of incense float around our house, coming from the temple buildings and the clothes of visitors who pass through the courtyard after praying. One of my housemates is learning to play the flute.

This night we have to keep the houses dark. From the house next door, I hear someone playing music and loud, off-key singing and laughing. We are playing poker at our own house, but quietly, our windows blacked out for the national nighttime emergency drill.

82

AMERICAN FACE

THE EWHA WOMEN'S UNIVERSITY FESTIVAL begins today. My friend's sister, who I met with our Russian group, is meeting me there with her classmates. We have a good time watching the activities, and we explore the campus. It is an old university for Korea, initially a study center founded by an American missionary, a woman from Smith College in 1886, then named a school by King Kojong in 1887.

We want to visit a friend in one of the Ewha University dorms, but no visitors are allowed, so we have ice cream with her in the exterior lobby instead. I have to leave early to be in time for Korean class ... for which only three students show up. Since we are so few, our teacher takes us back to the festival.

The art students are drawing portraits to raise money for their club, so a couple of us let them try our faces. Mine turns out to be a gross caricature of a western face: long forehead and jaw, with round, down-turned eyes, and a very long, pointed nose. My features, yet not. Our teacher is mad, and doesn't want me to pay. She says, it is ugly and doesn't look like me at all. It wasn't supposed to be a caricature, but the art student is new, and probably has very little experience with western faces so we compromise, and I pay half—respecting my teacher but also appreciating the student's effort.

83

PIZZA

AFTER THE FESTIVAL, we go out for pizza at one of the rare pizza houses.

Our teacher usually manages to pay for the meals or beer when we go out, so this time we very carefully maneuver her to sit in the corner where she cannot easily get out to pay. But it turns out that, as we are cleverly discussing how to keep her from paying, she has already outsmarted us by giving her credit card to the waitress as we walk in. She wins again. It is a constant game, to see who gets to pay.

Typically the older person should pay, up to a point, or the senior among juniors. It is an intricate game of insistence to win the bill for a dinner. It can be awkward when an American gets into the mix because we don't quite understand the particular long-term reciprocity of it, nor the delicate balance of respect and insistence that goes into it.

84

COURTYARD

WHILE IT IS STILL DARK this morning before the chanting begins, the crying of the puppy wakes me up. He is lonely and knows so many people are nearby. I squeeze my eyes shut and wait for someone to take care of him but I don't hear anyone stir. He paws at the step that runs along the front of our rooms but is too small to jump up.

Not able to bear the sound of his distress any longer, I get out of bed and go out into the empty courtyard. I pet and quiet him. We play for a while, but it is very cool in the predawn, my pajamas are lightweight, and I am getting cold. He has been allowed sometimes into a side room near the kitchen, so I open that door a little and give the puppy a foot up. He runs in and curls up on a floor pillow, content. I quietly slide the door closed and return to my own room.

As I open the door to my room, the senior monk of our temple enters the courtyard from his room. He stops when he hears me slide open my door.

He can hardly see me because it is dark, but asks, "Crystal?"

"Ney" (Yes), I answer. Then he seems to be looking around for the now-quiet puppy, so I let him know that the dog is in the sitting room. Satisfied, he returns to his room. I hope he doesn't think I am just coming home. My reputation is tenuous enough as it is.

When I first moved in, this monk was concerned that I know what the facilities are like; wanting to make sure I would not be too shocked that they are not what I am used to, and thus, in my surprise, want to leave. I hear that he asks about me occasionally, to see how—or what—I am doing. He and I almost never see each other because the hours we keep are so different. It is several hours yet before we will be woken up for breakfast, but he will be at the main temple for meetings and prayers by then.

85

FESTIVAL

MY COUSIN RETURNS to the States tomorrow. It reminds us how far we are from family when someone leaves. To cheer me up, the Student Monk offers to take us downtown to find gifts for her to take home. Our route takes us back to the Ewha festival, which is in its final day.

At first, we only plan to pass through, but we are stopped by an intense public drama performance. The theme is a popular one—democratization and unification—this time with an extra emphasis on the need to throw off the American imperialist yoke.

The student actors dance and perform like professionals. The intensity of emotion, both among the players and the audience, is tangible. We are almost in tears of rage and embarrassment ourselves at the atrocities they are condemning, and find ourselves clapping for the performers, too.

My cousin and I are the only two white foreigners in the crowd, sitting almost oblivious to our own visibility as people shout anti-American slogans in response to the performance. We are two yellow heads in a crowd of a thousand people watching emotionally charged anti-American (anti-Western) drama.

There are some momentary glares from bystanders; but we are soon forgotten as attention is drawn back into the performances. The Student Monk begs us to leave as the mood intensifies, and we slip away just before it is over. My housemates worry about me and tell me to be more careful.

86

YANKEE GO HOME

S HORTCUTS ARE ALL TOO OFTEN longer than a simple detour. Or worse as I learned last night.

It takes a small knot of bravery—or foolishness—to venture one's yellow head onto a campus lined with anti-imperialist banners, preceding a likely demo which needs only a spark to set it into motion. Especially after yesterday's drama performance. And one's bravery feels even more like stupidity when one blunders into the midst of this tension only because it was a shortcut to a social rendezvous. Many of the banners hung on buildings and fences read "Yankee, Go Home!"

There are more peaceful and even more scenic ways to reach the other side of Yonsei's main gate: around, for instance. But of course, the other ways are not nearly so direct or interesting as going straight through the center of campus, and it isn't until actually in the presence of a gathering demonstration that one can feel how close it is to happening. It is not difficult to find oneself in a demo as it builds and begins, especially as they grow more and more frequent.

Some students smile and say "hello," while others glare at me. In general, they don't treat me as if I, personally, am the cause of their troubles. My government, they know, is bigger than one citizen, and this one is a student guest in their country. Most of them ignore me, as they have bigger issues at hand—studies as well as saving their country—than a foreigner walking by.

As I approach the main gate I can see, just inside, a great crowd of people gathered. When I get closer, I finally feel the tension between police and students, and through the gate's iron bars I can see the sun gleaming off rows of black helmets. There are a few hundred riot police standing maybe ten feet from the gate, facing the students, not moving. Inside, their student counterparts sit in hundreds of small groups, dressed in T-shirts and jeans, bandanas ready to pull up over their faces when the tear gas begins.

From what I can understand of the banners and a few words caught here and there, it is to be an anti-president Roh and anti-American demo today. It is a huge demonstration because of the approaching anniversary of the Kwangju Massacre on May 18, 1980—also known as *oh-il-pal*, or the 518 Democratization Movement, according to a Korean custom of describing an incident by the date it happened. The Korean War, for example, is often referred to as *Yuk-i-oh*, or 625—the first day of the war.

Nine years of having the government try to cover up their violence and oppression is nowhere near long enough for families, friends, or anyone in this country to have forgotten what happened, and the protests against it are growing as the date approaches. The biggest demonstrations may be yet to come.

The reason for my shortcut is to meet the Russian study group, for which it is too easy to be late. In spite of my hurry I give in to common sense, turn around, take a detour, and am late once again—but at least I make it there.

My friends and I can't avoid being caught up in the intensity of the day. We have an unusually open discussion in a mixture of Russian, English, and Korean, talking about the demos, politics, history, Kwangju, and the United States. Most days we are reticent to discuss these topics in public, perhaps in fear of being overheard discussing dangerous topics—dangerous if the wrong ears decide they need someone new to arrest, but today we don't care. But when I quietly offer them my Manifesto copy, however, they sit back and shake their heads, quickly changing the topic. This, more than anything, brings it all home to me, and I realize what a risk we took. I hope all those wrong ears were busy dealing with demonstrations today.

87

NIGHT POLICE

ACCORDING TO THE RUMORS flying throughout campus today, the largest demonstration yet is planned for tomorrow, the actual anniversary of the Kwangju massacre, on the 18th, nine years ago. In spite of all the protests so far, the government still won't take responsibility for what they did. People are growing more angry that their government can act against its own people. And they fear that, as long as the government officials can ignore it, pretend they did nothing wrong, it could happen again. The campus is humming with energy like a hive of bees. Angry bees.

In the early evening, after a long day of classes and tutoring, then a simple dinner full of discussions of current events with friends, I'm finally headed home toward campus—but policemen choke the streets and subway entrances at the university stop, armed with batons and dressed in riot gear. Holding lists of wanted students, they examine everyone who passes, stopping some and letting the rest of us pass by. They don't confront me at all.

Once out of the subway near campus, I see they've blocked the roads to the university. Taking the roads that head toward the temple entrance past campus on the right, I find their parked riot buses have completely jammed the street to the temple and the mountain, too. It's getting late, but I don't feel safe passing through, so I turn around and walk back around it all to my parents' house on the other side of campus at the Foreign School. It's a long way, but it feels safer. By the time I get there, it is already dark.

I expect I can safely get home from there, avoiding the university altogether by taking the mountain trail. My parents are relieved to see me. I am so late that with the blockades my housemates have called to see if I'm safely there with them. When I call back to say I'm planning to head over, my housemates try to dissuade me. I insist I'm comfortable going over the mountain in the dark, and I never encounter police there at night. I assume the police are all on the roads and focused on the front gate of campus. At last, they agree but insist I wait for an escort. I put on my black coat, tuck my hair into a black cap, and wait just outside the back gate of the Foreign School compound.

I know the path well enough to walk without a light when I cross the mountain on my way home at night, and I wear the black cap and coat to be less visible to anyone possibly lingering there in the dark. As a woman alone, and as an American amidst the current protests against American policy, I want to have the element of surprise on my side. The wind rustling the grasses makes more noise than I do.

My housemates have sent the Student Monk. On the way over, he tells me, he found some riot police staked out on the mountain for the night. I can tell he is reluctant to take me back, but it would be awkward for him to stay at our house, and I imagine it can't be that bad to pass by the police with a monk at my side. Anyway, he made it here safely. So we head back.

The mountain is intensely dark, and a light wind makes the bushes rustle. There should be a bright, nearly full moon, but it is covered by clouds. What light there is does not penetrate the trees. I know the trail better, so I lead. Silently, we head out, along a side trail, and up the slope. On the way to the temple, we are stopped three times.

When we reach the break in the wire-topped wall which marks the border of the university grounds, I feel a dangerous tension in the air, but still don't see or hear any police. I hope they have left, and we can get home without any encounters.

The Student Monk steps forward to go over the wall first, but I shake my head. I'm the one who has put us at risk. I step onto the leaning branch and begin to climb over, hoping the police haven't come up this far, if they are still around. The branch creaks and I hear voices shout out in alarm. Beams of light swivel toward me from over the wall, and I finally, dreadfully, fully understand what a bad idea this was. Now it is too late to go back.

The cut coils of barbed wire on either side of me throw scar-like shadows over my hands and clothes as I top the cement wall. The semicircle of flashlights blinds me and the police shout at me in Korean, "Stop!" "Who are you?!"

What can I say? After a pause one sharply orders, "Come down!"

The Student Monk whispers urgently from behind, "Show your hair!"

Still atop the wall, I slowly raise one hand to my head and remove the black watch-cap. My blond hair tumbles over my shoulders and down my back, momentarily shocking the

222

police into silence. I hear startled murmurs, "A woman? A foreigner?"

It is not lost on me that, blond foreigner or not, being dressed in black and climbing through cut barbed wire does not make me look like an innocent guest returning home to her boarding house. Fear makes me want to freeze, or run, but instead I calm my breath, try to descend the wall without stumbling, and hide the shaking of my hands and knees.

My housemate could have stayed hidden, but he follows me over the wall. Although I am sure he is as afraid as I am, when he reaches the ground, he faces the police with as much authority as they have barked at us.

In Korean he gives his name and rank in the special forces, and they take notice. He continues, "You know I am a monk at this temple now!" He points across the mountain. He continues to speak as forcefully as if he outranks them, which he may, for all I know.

The police look nervous, but I'm not sure they quite believe him. He is young for his declared rank, and wearing jeans and a light jacket like a student, neither uniform nor monk's robes, though his head is shaved like a monk's. In an unfortunate coincidence, however, student dissidents have shaved their heads bald this week, like his.

The police surround and close in on us, and I follow his example: keep breathing, not ragged gasps that would show my fear, but calm, calm ... An officer finally steps forward. He is angry, shouting in our faces. It doesn't seem like this is the one who gave the Student Monk permission to pass on the way here. We stand very still, not flinching.

But then an even higher-ranking officer enters the circle of flashlights, shuts him up and slowly, coldly, his gaze travels over us as he takes in the details of our features, our clothes, our composure. The police are all silent, and we do not move. At last, he scoffs and turns away, dismissing us with a wave of his hand. We are free to pass but he offers no escort.

I feel an intense relief as we step away from them, but at a sudden break in the clouds, the moonlight reveals for a moment the black outlines of hundreds of policemen gathered, lining the narrow roadway down the hill to the temple where we live. I glance at my companion's face and realize there must be more here now than when he came to get me an hour ago. Then the moon is gone, and the mountain is dark again. The rank smell of sweat and alcohol reaches my nose.

The peril of our situation returns to me, and my breath bursts out like a short laugh. My housemate looks at me sharply. He is fully aware of the danger we are in and he does not find it funny. I do not tuck my hair back into the cap but let it fall inside my coat instead of down my back, less visible yet without looking like I'm trying to hide. I try to give no sign of the fear that makes my knees nearly buckle and, trembling inside, I step forward with him onto the path.

We pass the first group without incident. In the darkness, perhaps they can't see us well enough to realize that we are not soldiers, or maybe they just don't want to get involved unless they are told to. Then we are stopped at a turn in the road as the moon briefly breaks free from the clouds again. On either side the police stand up and move together, blocking the road. There is no way to go but toward them, through them. As we get closer, they can see—even in the darkness—that one of us is a foreigner and the other is not a soldier. Again, they slowly circle around us, and this time the smell of soju is strong. I quietly clench my teeth and my fists under my long coat sleeves, yet try to appear relaxed.

This time there is no officer to tell them they can let us go. Somehow the Student Monk convinces them that they don't want to interfere with a foreigner—she's unlikely to be a dissident, and it would just cause an international incident. With no officer to take charge, they mutter, but finally step aside.

Once they let us go, we are almost free. We can see lights on in our house at the bottom of the hill. There are smaller groups of soldiers on the trail ahead of us, between us and home. Only one group seems to have any inclination to stop us, and the alcohol smell of soju is even stronger than before. They move into the road. We walk on as if we have the right to. They seem less organized, uncertain whether to confront or stop us, but we have clearly been allowed to pass by everyone else, so they let us go on. Even so, one of them stumbles over to bump into me as I go by. I instinctively fling out my arm to push him away, then am immediately afraid of how the tension might explode if I hit him. But he is already gone in the darkness, and my hand passes through empty air.

Somehow, we make it into the courtyard. I bow quietly in thanks, but the Student Monk says nothing and goes directly to his room. I slide open my door and step over the wooden threshold onto the cool linoleum. The noise of the sliding door alerts a concerned housemate to poke his head out of his room. The Flute Player asks if I am all right.

Shaking now, and exhausted, I can only answer "Yes," and I close my door.

88

MORNING FANTASY

IT IS ALMOST FIVE A.M. NOW, and the memory of last night jolts me awake. But all the sounds outside my rice paper door are normal, as if nothing had happened. The temple is already alive with the day. The main temple bell has been gonging, and a small handbell is ringing somewhere. Hikers are already on the top of the mountain, yodeling to the dawn. The memory of going over the mountain last night plays back in my mind like a nightmare, and I cannot go back to sleep. The darkness under the obscured moon left the images so vague in my mind that it takes a conscious effort to make sense of it, to remind myself that it wasn't just some sort of ghost story, but really happened.

I dress and prepare for class silently, without my usual bright face. My housemates respect my quiet demeanor, and we don't joke with each other this morning. But the Flute Player mentions to no one in particular, slowly, and just loud enough that I can hear, that the police are gone, departed sometime in the night, before dawn. I can't imagine why they'd be gone, but I am used to not knowing why things happen, now.

At breakfast, I notice that they leave the apple cubes from the fruit salad on the plate, knowing those are my favorite bits, and I feel their care for me.

A few hours later I am walking over the mountain to class and last night seems to be even more of only a dream. Or maybe this morning is just an illusion. Sometimes the mountain seems to play with us, as if time moves differently there, offering us memories or maybe making us forget.

The mountain is full of ordinary people this morning, no sign that there were ever police here. The sun is bright, and families are hiking or playing badminton. Beekeepers are dozing near their hives as usual, and water gatherers are filling containers at the wells. The sunbeam shines through the trees, illuminating the little Mountain Spirit shrine. The scenes are so enchanting that they might have been painted to illustrate a fairy tale. I look and cannot find even one boot print of a soldier in the dust on the dirt road.

Tentatively crossing through the same barbed wire-topped wall as the night before, I feel that two contrasting worlds are existing in the same space. As I reach the top, checking to make sure the other side is clear, an uncle calls out, "You can't go there!" I am startled, and turn, but the old man just smiles teasingly at me as if we share a secret no one else knows, and waves me on. As I drop to the other side I look back at him again, but he isn't there, gone like a mountain spirit, another crossover between the different realities of this mountain.

JUNE 1, 1989

—

JUNE 14, 1989

89

EXAM WEEK

C LASSES ARE OVER AT LAST. We have finished all our exams and turned in our final papers. So much studying and work, I couldn't even write in my journal. I feel like sleeping for a week. I think I will.

And I think I know what happened with the police last week, why they disappeared. The Kwangju demos became so huge, they involved the entire city. Detaining a few student dissidents sneaking in the back door of our university turned out to be the least of their worries.

It seems there are several parts to the protests. The dramatic part is the tear gas and Molotov cocktails, or bottle bombs. This is what we see in the news. Then there are the protestors with signs expressing what they need addressed, what they want to change. And then there are those who aren't on the streets, but behind the scenes negotiating, or working out how to implement those changes—not just what the people don't want, but what they want to see instead. Or in the case of a leader or policy, not just to remove and leave a vacuum, but to have a better solution ready to put in place.

And all of it is framed for the public by whoever is reporting it, showing it in the light they want people to see. Some of the news channels pretty much tell it like it is, which is what they want people to see; other news channels show camera angles to make one side look more violent or ridiculous, for example, and the other to look more righteous, whether they really are, or not. We are learning to tell the difference. The week looked like this:

KOREA HERALD   MAY 24, 1989

150 students, riot policemen injured in Kwangju clashes

The fiercest clash during a week of rallies to observe the ninth anniversary of the May 18 civil uprising occurred when about 2,000 Chonnam University students and citizens attempted to break through a cordon of riot troopers blocking their march in front of the provincial capital building in the evening. The demonstrators, chanting anti-government and anti-American slogans, began to throw rocks and pieces of paving stones at the riot troopers, who hurled them back ... At least 40 students and citizens and 110 policemen were reported injured in the battle for control of the city's main plaza, symbolic center of the 1980 uprising in which nearly 300 [sic] civilians were killed by armed troops.

90

ACUPUNCTURE

THE ARTIST WHO ARRANGED for me to stay at the temple has returned to our house for a visit, staying in the now empty room next to mine. I've hardly seen her, though, because I'm sleeping and she is catching up with her friends and always out somewhere. I get a feeling of what I must seem like to my housemates as I watch her trying to do too much, to get the most out of every day here, returning home late, exhausted, and moaning about how it takes forever to get anywhere in the city. Like me.

Now I have time to take my housemates' advice to get acupuncture treatment. They tell me I look too tired and pale, and that I don't eat enough. I know I look pale, but I've tried to tell them my color is normal for a European, not a sign of poor health. But they are right: I shouldn't have such dark circles under my eyes.

I don't really know what to expect, besides needles, but I'm willing to try. On Sunday, the doctor comes to the temple to see me for the first time and plans to work on me every morning at eight a.m. for a week.

What is an acupuncture exam? For this first visit, especially, she feels my back, hands, stomach, feet, legs; she checks my tongue and eyes. Then she ion-beams my hands and puts needles in them, for about fifteen minutes in one hand, twenty-five minutes in the other. During that time, she uses a hot, glowing wooden tool, or *moxa*, to heat points on my hands. This is called "hand acupuncture," a method recently developed in Korea. She tells me that my body is "cold," so I have to sleep with a hot water bottle and to keep warm at all times. I don't feel cold in this June heat, but apparently this is a constitutional concept, not a thermometer temperature.

Eastern medicine is concerned with, among other things, the balance of heat and cold in the body. She admonishes me to get plenty of good sleep and to eat well, three times per day, at regular hours, and 'no ice cream.' My mother has been telling me the same thing for years, though she is a little more relaxed about the ice cream.

91

RICE GLUE OR ... WINE

THE LEFTOVER RICE PASTE from about a month ago that I kept to glue paper onto my steamer trunk has since become accidental rice wine. Kind of.

Actual rice wine is called *makkoli*. It's a slightly cloudy and lightly alcoholic traditional beverage, best drunk with friends on rainy days. Or any time, but with friends. We learned this from our Korean teacher, who took us out to a makkoli house instead of class one rainy day so we could experience the real thing in the best atmosphere: a traditional wooden-beamed tavern where the *makkoli* is served in pottery bowls along with green onion pancakes.

The kind of rice paste in the jar on my shelf, before it gets fermented, makes an excellent glue for pasting paper onto the old rusty trunk that I am using for storage in my room.

I found an old paintbrush to apply the glue after it cooled: strategically cutting and pasting colorful rice paper

I bought in Insa-dong to cover the rust and mars on the trunk. This is a big piece of furniture for my tiny room, so how it looks has a big impression on the room's atmosphere. It was dark and dirty-looking before, but now it brightens up my room. I restrain myself from papering the walls with the leftover varicolored paper.

92

SHAVEN

STUDENTS IN CHINA are protesting, too, along with workers and everyone. But today their government brought in the army and killed we don't know how many people who had been protesting in front of the Imperial palace at Tiananmen Square in Beijing. We don't know the details because we don't get much news from communist countries here, and if we do, it is sanitized and censored. A dictatorship, even one that was somewhat fairly elected like here in Korea, is clearly not much better than communism. It feels like the whole world is changing, with protests happening all around the globe. I hope democracy wins out.

Here in Korea the police are now detaining the students with shaved heads. Unfortunately, although the hair is beginning to grow back, their short hair easily identifies the more ardent protestors and makes them easy targets for the police. It is nearly impossible to arrest them when they are on campus protesting within the gates, because the university is supposedly sanctuary and off limits to the police, but they are easily identified off campus now.

Unfortunately, the Student Monk is also detained on his way home from his university. This time the police are rough and do not listen to him, like they did when we crossed the mountain. He does not have his monk ID on him, and he is dressed in plain clothes, so they do not believe his protests that he has short hair because he is a monk. They are sure he is lying. They toss him into a van and take him off to the police headquarters.

There they fingerprint him, and only become more angry when he continues to insist he is a monk. At last, the police chief comes. He checks out the "monk's" story, threatens to call the temple, thinking to call his bluff. The Student Monk agrees and gives him the phone number of the temple. The chief calls and finds that he is actually holding a monk, and the son of a head monk, at that.

Embarrassed, the police let him go, but the Student Monk is terribly humiliated and shaken. If the police chief had not shown up, who knows what could have happened. The abuses during arrests are often bad enough to make Amnesty International intervene: terrible torture and forced, false confessions can end in disappearance or confirmed death in police custody or after encounters with police.

In the way that the mundane gets mixed in with the unbearable, the police made the Student Monk miss the meeting he was headed to. The red ink from the fingerprinting will not wash off easily, making it shamefully obvious that he was arrested. He goes to my parents' house first, to try to wash off the ink. My parents feed him and tell him it's okay, that being wrongly arrested does not make you a criminal. Even if he had been protesting injustice, that would not have made him a criminal in their eyes.

93

OUR POSTER, MY FLAG

WALKING HOME FROM THE SUBWAY and through Yonsei campus, I see my red-headed American classmate and her blond Canadian boyfriend in front of the International Building. She is shaking, clearly upset, holding a large scrap of dirty, rumpled paper in her hand as she paces back and forth at the foot of the stairs. Her boyfriend tries to step toward her, speak to her, but she puts up a hand for him to stay back.

I stop to ask her if they're okay, though clearly they are not. She is trying to calm herself, she says, before she speaks with the Yonsei Dean of Students. I look at her boyfriend, and he shrugs. She raises her hand again and tells him, "This isn't your fight." I ask her what happened.

She has just had a confrontation with some of the Korean students. While walking back to her dormitory, she says, they came across a poster of a U.S. flag taped to the ground in front of the steps to a main building. Emblazoned across it in English was "Son of Bitch." Some of the students were intentionally stepping on it. When they noticed her watching, some of them stomped harder and checked to see her reaction. At last she could not stand it any longer, and walked over to tear the flag off the ground. A tug of war with a student ensued. Her boyfriend stepped forward to help her, but she was afraid he might be mistaken for an American and the students might fight with him so she had pushed him back yelling, "He's Canadian!" (which he is). She and the student continued shouting at each other, both trying to take the flag. Neither could understand the other, except when once the student shouted, "It's our poster!" and she answered, "It's MY flag!" When the flag poster ripped in half, her boyfriend caught her and the other students pulled their classmate back. They are waiting to speak with the dean, too, gathered at the other end of the stairs.

As her friend and fellow American, I join her, staying in the background as moral support when she meets with the Korean dean. He tells the students that he understands their concerns, but the radical groups should not insult the foreign students by defacing their flags and putting them on the ground to be walked on. The American students here in Korea are the ones who are most likely to form or change U.S. policy toward Korea in the future, he tells them, and it won't improve international relations to antagonize one another.

The students don't seem convinced, saying that the foreigners in the international division on campus remain aloof from the Korean students, don't even seem to care. Unlike me, most foreign students live in the international dormitory, and there is not much interaction or opportunity to make friends with the Korean students. Both sides are full of stereotypes and prejudices about the other.

The dean mediates and gets both parties to agree to meet again. Meanwhile, they are to come up with ideas for how Korean and foreign students on campus can interact, socialize, and at least talk with one another. He doesn't give them a date to return and report back.

On the way back to the dorm, I encourage her and her boyfriend to follow his advice. I am already interacting, socializing, and talking with Korean students every day, and can encourage them that it is worthwhile for all of us to cross that divide. I hope they do, but I doubt they'll have time to follow through. The semester is over, and foreign students have to move out of the dorms within the week.

94

CHINA

THIS ARTICLE MAY EXPLAIN why we don't know much about what is going on in China. One of the foreign students—Ron, who received his sparsely addressed mail so quickly—found an article from a Hong Kong Newspaper.

```
HONG KONG
SUNDAY MORNING POST          JUNE 25, 1989

Koreans muted over massacre

From LIZ McGREGOR in Seoul

    For once, Korean activist students have
acted in concert with their government. The
official reaction of both parties to the
massacre in China has been so muted as to be
virtually inaudible. The reasons, however, for
their indifference are profoundly different…
```

... A few days after the massacre on Tiananmen Square, the Foreign Ministry quietly issued a statement expressing. "regret" over the situation in China and "our earnest desire for the speedy restoration of peace and order."

Although South Korea has no official ties with China - one of North Korea's best friends - unofficial trade with China has boomed over the past couple of years ...

... Mr Rhee Sang-ho, editor of the English language newspaper at Yonsei University which has led student struggles for the past few years, explained it thus: "Students were very confused by what happened in China because they follow the ideas of Mao."

Another reason for the apparent lack of support, said Mr Rhee, was that Korean students were preoccupied with their own issues...

95

WARM HANDS

ACUPUNCTURE AGAIN TODAY. After the doctor has placed the needles in my hands and left me sitting alone in the meeting room, a monk walks in. I saw him at a temple ceremony a few weeks ago, and doing the drum dance on Buddha's Birthday. He also reads faces and hands. Greeting him properly is only partially possible. With about fifteen needles in each hand, I can't really get up or bring my hands together in front of my face, but I try, he waves me to stay sitting. The doctor returns soon after; they discuss me and my health.

The monk consults with her, then feels my hands and studies them. I am uneasy about being touched with all these needles in my hands, until my doctor reaches over and removes them. Then the monk holds his hands above mine—to give healing, he says. I can feel a heat spreading through my hands and arms. I feel revitalized after this visit, and my chronically cold hands are warm.

96

RUDE

THERE IS AN OLD MAN staying at our temple now, perhaps related to someone here. Or maybe just in need of a place to stay. He's fairly quiet but doesn't really seem to be comfortable here. I see him in the common room playing solitaire with some cards, and affectionately try to tell him that he reminds me of my own grandfather who also loves to play solitaire. He is angry at my forwardness and gives me a long, stern, and loud lecture on how to speak to my elders.

I am surprised and hurt, apologize for whatever transgression I've made, but can say no more. By this time, I am afraid to open my mouth. My Korean is so limited that I am sure to make some other serious error in manners or honorific level, or even in speaking at all.

Perhaps making him even angrier, I am trying to show him that I meant to be respectful by looking him in the eye the entire time he is speaking to me, just as I was taught as a child. In Korea, apparently, one should never stare in the face of parents or any senior lecturing you. You should stare at one's own feet or the floor or some other low place. My past training is automatic, with parents saying, "Look at me when I speak to you!" if a child dared look away as if they were not paying attention to the lecture. When he is finished, or taking a breath for more outburst, I say *mianhamnida* "I'm sorry" in the highest form I know, step backwards out of the room, slide the door closed, and escape.

JUNE 15, 1989

—

JUNE 30, 1989

97

MEDICINE

AIR RAID DRILL TODAY.
Fifteenth of the month, so the air raid siren wails across the city in the afternoon. It always makes my skin crawl, and I seek shelter from the sky along with the rest of the country. We are thoroughly reminded that North Korea could attack at any time. I'm not sure the threat is as strong as the reminder, though.

After tutoring on a hot Friday afternoon, I see the acupuncturist with her teacher. I've been so exhausted these days, as if I am living too many lives at once—mostly classes at the university, events at the temple, tutoring and modeling, study groups, invitations to go out with friends and acquaintances, running errands, and visiting my parents. I never feel as though I can decline. But one day I was so exhausted I fainted in a pizza parlor and had to go to the hospital. I don't keep my journal some days because, well, I am too exhausted.

When I meet the acupuncturist's teacher, I can't understand what he says or wants me to do because my "translator" friend hardly speaks English. He is frustrated to be unable to ask me questions. The teacher and my doctor discuss my case for a while, look over at me wilting in the heat, then the two of them go off to find refreshing drinks for all of us, along with the friend I've brought to try to translate for me. We are in a bungalow-type eating room just big enough for two tables and about twenty chairs packed tightly around them. They bring back bowls of a wonderful, iced drink with bits of fruit floating in it. I'm surprised she gives me ice.

When we are finished and refreshed, without any more discussion, the doctors arrange the chairs into a kind of cot for me. I lay down and the teacher doctor reads the pulses in my wrist. Then he presses his fingers into my abdomen, searching for the places that feel pain and those that do not. From this examination and the consultation with his student, he sends for some herbal medicine for me.

The medicine arrives in a huge box the next day: about one hundred bottles of the most horrible liquid concoction I have ever had to consider potable in my entire life. Once a whiff gets to my nose, I can hardly bring the bitter stuff to my lips. It should be wonderful medicine. I must take one bottle (about 8 ounces) warmed, three times a day.

98

HOLE IN THE WALL

THE MOUNTAIN IS DEPENDABLE, and my feet know the path even when my mind is elsewhere. The one thing that changes there is the wall.

Just when I thought the barbed wire was never repaired, they have started to repair it, making the wall very inconvenient to climb and slowing travelers down. They don't slow us down much, though, as it's easy enough to find a small detour leading to the bunker close enough to the wall that one can climb onto it and over the wall. It's a bit of a drop on the other side, but the wire there seems to have escaped notice and is not repaired.

Most of the time, we climb the branch or pile of cement blocks or stones to reach the top, in the spot where the barbed wire has been cut away, and easily drop down on the other side. It isn't a big secret: the cut is usually in a convenient place close to the path. But sometimes the branches and stones are scattered in the woods. If there is nothing to stand on, we have to work a little harder to pull ourselves over. But now that they are repairing the wire, it'll be less convenient.

Before long, however, we will have another alternative, closer to the main path. Someone has found a weak place in the wall and started a small demolition. Eventually it should make a hole just big enough to hunch through without actually crawling. Each time one of us passes this wall next to the bunker, we kick the same spot and the hole is growing. The ajoshi, or uncles, who climb the mountain for exercise or to collect water from the springs are particularly diligent, and seem to consider the wall a personal affront, taking their time to be sure they kick away a good piece of cement before they continue on. I kick at it, too, for good measure, though with little effect. The ajoshi smile at me and nod in approval anyway. Community effort and patient persistence will prevail.

99

THE COLOR OF DEATH

M Y LITTLE SIX-YEAR-OLD STUDENT is my teacher today. She is Korean-American, born in the states, but has moved to Korea with her family. Her mother wants her to go to the foreign school, and requires her to be able to read English at or above standard second grade level. When she came to me in April, she couldn't read at all. She is making very quick progress, so as a treat I prepare an illustrated story with her as the main character in an imaginary adventure. My student loves the pictures, especially.

I write each word in a different color to make reading easier and prettier, and she is drawn into the unfolding tale of a little girl just like her who has accidentally turned into a dragon. She must find a way to make her parents know it is her, so they can love her and she can become herself again. But at one point I write her name in dark pink. She is horrified and insists I must change the color. She explains that to write someone's name in red means death—that's how a person's death is recorded in the family book, in red ink.

After I remedy the problem by scratching off as much pink crayon as I can and writing over it in dark blue. She is satisfied and goes back to reading. She discovers that the parents know the dragon is their daughter when it writes a message to them. Her eyes twinkle and she laughs because she knows what I've done, but the story does its job and gives her new purpose and courage. She asks me to write more stories for her. "But please," she insists, "You must never write my name in red!"

I am delighted at her progress and ask her to read for her mother. In front of her mother, however, my little student suddenly stutters and can't make out the words. Her mother is clearly disappointed in her, and I wish I hadn't insisted.

100

MEDICINE ON THE METRO

I AM STUCK DOWNTOWN TODAY in rush hour on the crowded Seoul metro when the hour strikes to take my medicine. I've been keeping the glass bottle in a pocket against my body to warm it up. Luckily, I have a seat, but my stop is still half an hour away and I won't be able to get home for a few hours after that, so there is nothing to do but take it here and now.

The stares, when I pull that bottle out of my shirt, and people smell it, see a foreigner drinking traditional medicine even many of them wouldn't take ... I think I'm getting a perverse liking for the pungent herbs and this bewildered attention. When I look up and face all the people staring at me, they remember not to look and suddenly I am anonymous again. At least I can pretend so.

101

HELLO

TODAY ON THE MOUNTAIN path a student stops and calls out "Hello!" as I pass. I don't recognize him, so I answer quickly in Korean, barely glancing at him. He looks surprised but I don't stop, and I rush on by to class. Later, sitting at my desk, I realize he seemed familiar, a friend of one of my housemates. I've only met him once, maybe twice, but among a large group of guys visiting in the common room. Even so, he must have thought I was pretty rude.

I'm so used to strangers asking if they can practice English with me. It's happened more, since some people recognize me from the poster ads in shop windows. Sometimes I do: it can be fun. But not today. I didn't want to stop, or I'd be late to the lecture.

102

DMZ

I HAVE A CHANCE to join a tour to Panmunjom, the border negotiation village in the De-Militarized Zone, or DMZ, between North and South Koreas, and I take it. Panmunjom is quite a bit more secure than our little mountain, and you can only go with a scheduled tour, which is typically booked well in advance, but well worth the effort of trying to get in: you have to be approved. The U.S. army requests the passports of the visitors, and I understand light security checks are done once they get the list of names.

Included in the invitation is a dress code. Because the border village is always under surveillance by both North and South Korea, we tourists have to look good for the cameras so as not embarrass our host (South Korea). On the day of the tour we meet the large tour bus downtown, show our passports, pass scrutiny, and find our seats.

On the way north from Seoul, the guide points out various fortifications that are easy to overlook on a normal day, but that you can't miss once you've been told. Buildings at major intersections in the city have doors wide enough to permit a tank to enter and defend the intersections and streets. Outside the city, we see huge blocks suspended above the road that appear to be simply marquees for signage until the guide points them out. These can be dropped to block the highway where it is skirted by rice paddies so that tanks trying to get around would be mired in mud. The hilltops, she tells us, are ringed with cement walls and barbed-wire fences. The tourists look and nod, impressed; I make no comment about this detail.

South Korea's capital city is barely twenty-five miles from the border with North Korea. A leisurely two-day hike. But the road is not straight, or clear, and it is well over half an hour drive to get there. We pass through several security checkpoints. Exciting. Perhaps.

The guide points out that, because the war is not officially over, military service is compulsory. Almost every young Korean man—or his sister, I have heard, in some rare cases—has to perform military service soon after high school, and many work directly with the Americans as KATUSA (Korean Army Training with US Army). Most of my housemates have already served, though not with KATUSA, returning a couple of years later to finish university.

We are told to behave ourselves, as the North Koreans are eager to have any possible bad press of the south, even if it is only a poorly behaved or scantily dressed tourist. I suspect that the exceptionally good-looking soldiers on both sides are part of competition to impress, as well.

Panmunjom itself is a military compound more than a village. Through the middle of the compound runs a raised, cement curb: it marks the border, the armistice line drawn in the sand. The village is guarded by North Korean soldiers on one side, United Nation soldiers on the South, mostly American. They seem bored enough, but are very tense, ready for any irregularity. We are amply warned not even to approach the border line. Neither side would care whether you were a spy, a defector, or just crazy—you would be apprehended or shot if you tried to cross.

We also visit some of the underground tunnels, which supposedly connect North and South, and were dug, we are told, by the northern army trying to sneak south for an attack. Several of the tunnels have been discovered, and maybe some have not. We are escorted from the tunnels to a lookout building, complete with dioramas to show the terrain of the border for tourists, and 25-cent/100 *won* telescopes through which we can look at the soldiers in the north. I note that both coins are exactly the same size and weight, though the 100 *won* is only worth about ten cents.

Away from the negotiation village, the border becomes wide and more traditionally fortified. Soldiers, guns, barbed wire … Each side has erected slogans in huge white Hollywood style letters, which may be either to encourage sympathy or defectors, or to insist that this or that regime is the best. It seems dramatic, but the governments take these politics extremely seriously. A South Korean can be arrested for showing any communist sympathy or inclination.

I think of my carry-on, when I flew to Korea, with my copy of The Communist Manifesto. So glad they didn't search my handbag that day. I try to think of what to do with it. I'm not sure I want to take it back out with me, but am afraid to leave it anywhere here.

We watch videos and hear lectures giving a brief background of the war (1950-1953, continuing but at ceasefire), history about happenings at the border village (crossovers or fights), and about the restrictions and negotiations. A few ridiculous details ... each side has built a tower to raise its flag, towers that have been constantly reconstructed to be taller than that of the other side. Imagine flagpoles that look like they were designed by Mr. Eiffel. Of course, each side also wants the biggest flag, incongruously outsized against the backdrop of unpopulated, verdant hills. In the negotiating room, the same competition occurs on a smaller scale on the negotiating table, with the flag stands on either side of the border line, which continues into the building and as a red stripe down the center of the table. The posturing has slowed down now that a kind of equilibrium has been reached: the North's flag is higher, but the South's has a larger base to stand on.

As we line up to board the bus, we hear snatches of excited conversation from passing soldiers about "her" coming here to the DMV. Judging by the welcome banners we see them unfurl, the next visitor after us is going to be Miss America. I wonder if we'll pass her on the road. On the return to Seoul, we again go through the array of security checkpoints, now aware of the fortifications, but we don't see Miss America.

103

"HANDSOME" OR "UGLY"

HOW DO YOU TAKE BACK the wrong words?
The Flute Player knocks on my door today. He is shy and a little uncertain, even though he is the senior student in our house, next to the PhD Candidate. I open the door and gasp in appreciation. He is all dressed up in a suit, his shoes polished and his hair neatly combed with maybe a little gel to hold it in place. He looks great.

He gestures at himself and turns around, almost blushing. He looked at me, questioningly, "Okay?"

He has come to me, the only female student in the house, for approval. I want to tell him he looks handsome. I want to use the most polite form I know. Often the polite form of a word is longer than the casual, so instead of saying the short *"Mossiseyo,"* I make it longer by saying "M*ossangyoseyo!"* with great enthusiasm.

His face falls in disappointment and resignation, he nods sadly, and sighs in Korean, *"Ney, arraso."*"Yes, I knew it."

I have mixed up the two Korean words and just told him he is ugly. All my protests that it isn't what I meant to say just seem to be me pretending I haven't accidentally spoken the truth in my mind. So I have to accept that I have just sent him off on one of his very rare dates with his confidence dragging in the dust behind him.

JULY 1, 1989

—

JULY 14, 1989

104

MOUNTAIN PATH

A ND I COME HOME LATE AGAIN.
I feel most alive crossing this mountain at night. There is no light, but I pass this way so often, I don't need it. My hands reach out to skim the rough bark of the trees as I pass. Even in the dark night my feet know the path. I round a tree, going up a small knoll: three steps ahead will be a rock in the path, buried deep, with just the top three inches showing above the soil, like an iceberg. My left foot steps just to the side of it every time.

I know each turn and dip in the path, duck under a low-hanging branch. Even during the daytime, I sometimes follow a game I used to play as a child on the wooded trails behind our home: closing my eyes for several steps—or more—to see if I really do know my way. I quickly learned distances feel different when my eyes are closed, and to trust my feet: confidently keep the same swing and length of stride or my steps will fall on an unfamiliar bump in the trail.

I enjoyed reading biographies when I was little—I still do—and may have gotten this idea from trying to understand Helen Keller. Living in a boarding house, where I can barely understand the conversations, instructions, or even find the words to ask questions helps me understand a little of what it feels like to be deaf and dumb. The dark mountain challenges me to see without my eyes, and I am grateful to Helen for her example of competence.

105

ELDER MONK

S EVERAL MONKS GATHER to watch in the room where I am receiving acupuncture. But it seems they are not just watching; they have something on their mind. They are animated, gesturing towards me as they talk. The elderly artist monk, the National Treasure Man-Bong Sunim, sits aside a bit, calm and perhaps bemused. He is studying me from under his bushy eyebrows as the acupuncturist places needles in my hands.

At last, he clears his throat. The others stop and turn to him, suddenly silent. He looks at me intently for a moment longer, gives a small nod, and turns to them. He speaks quietly, and I can't hear well or understand what he says. Then the monks turn to stare at me, still silent. The elderly artist monk gets up with his cane, waving aside the monks who lean forward to help him. He comes over to me, smiles, pats my shoulder, and putting one arm behind his slightly

269

curved back, the other on his cane, he elegantly leaves the room. The gathered monks give me one last, pausing glance, and follow him out.

I'm left sitting alone in the room with my hands full of needles, wondering what just happened.

106

MOUNTAIN SPIRIT

I FINALLY HAVE A CHANCE to ask the Student Monk if he knows why the monks came into the acupuncture room. What were they worried about, and what did the Elder Monk say to them?

It turns out, he tells me, they were worried about me being alone on the mountain at night. Korean mountains are haunted by so many spirits of those who died there—resistance fighters, soldiers, families, despondent lovers—as well as live people who might take advantage of a lone woman. At least, sadly but luckily, there are no more tigers to eat stray wanderers.

When I pass along the mountain paths, I haven't felt afraid, apart from that night when the mountain was full of police. I am cautious, of course, aware of bushes someone could hide behind, and I am alert to sounds that could be someone nearby, or the smell of alcohol or sweat. Sometimes

271

I hear the soft rustle of the grass near me as I walk, but too soft to be a person, more as if someone or something ethereal is gently walking beside me. In the morning I won't remember the whole walk home. It is as if I walked it in a dream. Is it only a dream that I have ever had any life but Korea, and the temple, and the mountain?

It turns out that the elder monk told the other monks not to worry; that the Mountain Spirit has been walking with me.

107

LATE AGAIN

S LEEPING AS A STUDY BREAK is a respectable hobby for serious students, and I do my best to practice it when I have a chance.

Tonight, at our house is the Youngest Guy's birthday, so my housemates wake me up from my evening nap to make sure I can participate in the party. We have a pink cake for him, and a knife to slice it, but we don't have plates or forks. So we all dig into the cake with chopsticks. As we stuff our mouths, we talk about going to the latest Indiana Jones movie. None of us has seen it, and the ads look exciting, so we decide to go.

The guys want to see the 11pm showing, which is too late for me—so we bargain about the time as if shopping in the market. I finally compromise that, if they can persuade another friend to go at that time, then I will go, too. Then they find out that the movie starts even later than they thought, so I completely decline. I am so sleepy that I know

I won't be able to function tomorrow, coming home at two in the morning. Besides, after hearing them discuss how late I often stay out, I want at least to pretend to prove them wrong.

So, we make a split-second decision, they gobble up the last of the cake while I slip back to my room to change into outside clothes, and we run to catch the temple bus downtown just in time for the nine o'clock movie. We don't make it home until after midnight, anyway, but at least it isn't two a.m.

What a great time. We have to walk home because all the buses have stopped, so we entertain ourselves by singing loudly in the streets. Luckily, most of the way home is not residential, and no one yells at us. Only a couple of policemen are there to raise their eyebrows at our racket.

And this time my accomplices can't ask why I am out so late.

108

SWASTIKA

A MAJOR SYMBOL FOR BUDDHISM—as the six-pointed star for Judaism, the cross for Christianity, and the crescent for Islam—is a whirling cross, a swastika. The name of the symbol derives from Sanskrit meaning, among other things, "all is well" or "welfare." It is commonly regarded as a symbol of good luck.

Inexplicably, Hitler took the symbol for his mark: supposedly and weirdly because he wanted a symbol of Aryanism, which comes from the 15th century B.C. people that conquered northern India. Even in the Americas and throughout Asia, however, it is an ancient and sacred symbol. He gave it a new meaning in the western world horribly opposite to the peaceful, life-respecting precepts it represents in Buddhism.

The Korean word for it, *manja,* I'm told, means "everything" (such as all creatures). *Man* (10,000) standing

275

for "everything," and *ja* "things". Literally 10,000 things. "Everything is as it is."

Now, seeing the symbol painted under the eaves of temple buildings in Asia can be a source of shock to tourists, even when they hear the religious meaning.

In reverse, it is surprising to Buddhists that westerners don't feel comfortable accepting gifts that are clearly marked with the whirling cross. They don't readily make the connection between their cross of creation and the Nazi mark of destruction. One of my friends wants to buy me a necklace with it as a pendant, and I have to beg her not to. I can't help but feel the horror of WWII in the back of my mind when I see it, and there is no way I can ever wear it, even if I appreciate the ancient meaning and the thought of the gift.

109

HOUSEMATES

"NEW HOUSE RULES," suggested the Flute Player last night: "Early getting up and early going to bed! We can play tennis or badminton on the mountain." That was last night. So now it is not quite 7:00 a.m., and we have all been woken up. I am already awake, fortunately, but not the guys. I jokingly wonder how long this guy will live if he keeps this up: longer than the rest of us if he keeps such good habits, but one of these days he is going to catch the others with a hangover, and then ...? I hope that doesn't happen too soon, because he is usually so sweet. Especially after my faux pas with mixing up handsome and ugly, for which he seems to have forgiven me, I'd hate to see him daunted. He keeps the rest of us in better spirits. But we do not go to play badminton on the mountain.

Later today I'll have to make reservations for the flight back to the United States. It feels like arranging a flight to some other planet.

JULY 15, 1989

—

JULY 31, 1989

110

STREET VENDORS

AIR RAID DRILL TODAY.
Waiting just inside a shop for the all-clear, the gossip is that street vendors are going to be outlawed.

Could such a law really work? And why? For today, vendors are still lining the streets, selling trinkets, snacks, jewelry, meals, clothes ... what would the city be without them—the surge of energy compressing every rush to work, class, meeting friends, leaving barely enough room for pedestrians to crowd by so that we jostle and interact, feel alive? How will we get those last-minute gifts, that quick snack to keep us going? The city will be nude without them.

The siren ends, pedestrians flood back onto the sidewalks, traffic moves again, and I catch my bus. Looking out the window at the bustling street business, I think about them. Would it even be Seoul?

When I get to the office building to teach my English class with salary men and women, I ask my students about the law.

The vendors will fight a ban, they tell me, or ignore it. Vending is how they earn money to feed their families. And pedestrians will resent it as their stomachs grumble and there is nothing easy to buy for the long ride home. What will we do when we are craving sweet or savory snacks from the vendor with a steel drum oven on a pull-cart? What will we do when we didn't bring an umbrella, the sky bursts with rain, and the umbrella vendor is gone ... or when the winter wind blows down our necks and we need a scarf against the cold ... or a handkerchief to wipe away the summer sweat? Where will we find flowers or a small gift for a friend we are meeting at the other end of the bus line? Or when we need a new pen? And what about the day workers who can't get home until late, but can't afford a restaurant meal? We rely on these street vendors all day. The law won't last.

They tell me that there are more than twenty thousand "illegal" street vendors, and the government wants to crack down because they are too difficult to tax. If the vendors protest—and they certainly will—the government will have to back down. Small people have great power, and sometimes the government needs to be reminded.

111

LIGHTS OUT

THE ELECTRICITY HAS GONE OUT, so I'm writing by the light of a gifted candle that has a love poem written on it in Korean. At least that's what my housemates tell me it is. Every little gift in the shops seems to have some sweet phrase on it, occasionally in English. This one is in *hangul,* Korean script, and cursive, so I can only make out the written word for love. Usually, I light temple candles when the lights go out, but now I have this one. Perhaps this is a subtly suggested alternative that I should save the temple candles for prayer.

The lights may be out for technical reasons, or it may be another drill for blacking out the country in case of air attack—in which case I shouldn't be using a candle since my rice paper windows don't have curtains. No one tells me to put it out.

112

SILENT CRAFT

B ECAUSE OF MY LACK of spoken language skills, I have become rather adept at talking with gestures and facial expressions. Today this comes in handy.

My mother, as school librarian, is preparing for the upcoming school year. She has invited me to help her on a shopping trip to buy literature-themed decorations for the school library: wall hangings, puppets and stuffed toys based on books that the children love. The ride is also a good chance for us to catch up with one another, since our paths so rarely cross.

Our destination is Silent Craft, a sewing factory she says was built by and for the deaf community with both local and international donations, to support themselves and be self-sufficient since they can't easily get jobs.

Mom is driving the school van, so we don't have to take a return taxi with all the boxes of decorations she is purchasing. She is very brave. Foreign teachers are divided

on whether they will drive in the wild traffic of Seoul—
either they love the challenge, or they refuse to chance it.
My mother loves the challenge. The traffic seems to make
way for her, even the taxis. She herded cattle as a kid and is
not intimidated by the chaos.

When we arrive at the gate, we are greeted by Sister
Caritas, the elderly but very lively German Benedictine
Catholic nun who is not deaf but serves the deaf
community. She gives us a tour of the warehouse. I am
entranced by the soft sewn crafts, mostly depicting fairy
tale characters and imaginary creatures. My mother is
looking especially for her student's storybook characters.

I look around at one point and find that I am alone. My
mother and Sister Caritas have moved on, leaving me
inattentively wandering the maze of shelves filled with happy
toys and decorations. It feels as though I've wandered into
the workshop of Santa's elves. I continue to amuse myself
with browsing, confident I'll find the others soon enough or
else be recruited to help prepare for Christmas.

Eventually I come out into an open space. In the break
between sections of shelves is an open workshop with about
eight of the real toy makers: members of the community
gathered for a break among their sewing machines. We
stare at each other for a moment, then begin to talk. I don't
know any formal sign language, but I remember my best
friend from kindergarten, who was deaf, and how we used
to talk. To their inquisitive glances, I explain myself using
gestures, and tell them how I have come to be lost.

They laugh and gesture to reassure me. Sister Caritas
and my mother will come back and find me here; I can stay
with them. We continue this way, talking about family: I
put my hand above my head, then to one side four steps
taller, to the other side three steps smaller to show where I
stand among my siblings. They explain who they are,

whether they are married, how many children they have. We discuss where we are from, this warehouse and workshop, life, demos, and politics; somehow it seems we can discuss anything. Some of them are local, some from the islands, others from orphanages or sent here by parents to get an education at the school and to have a job, a community.

They show me how they design new products, from imagination or books and stories, and then bring them into being with their sewing machines.

Eventually my mother and Sister Caritas come to find me. They are concerned I might have been worried about being lost, so I tell them, speaking aloud and gesturing as I have been, that we were all having a good conversation. The women laugh and agree. My mother and Sister Caritas are pleasantly surprised. I don't want to leave, but we must.

I am amazed at what a relief it is to be able to talk so freely! Why can we communicate so much better without spoken words, when language seems such a barrier between people who can hear perfectly well? We clasp hands with one another, saying goodbye.

In the taxi on the way home, my mother explains that Sister Caritas, who must be in her seventies by now, came to what is now North Korea as a missionary before WWII during the Japanese occupation. There she was asked to teach some deaf children to read and write. Living in Korea under the Japanese, she learned to speak Japanese, then Russian in a POW camp during WWII, then English in South Korea after the Korean War, and of course she speaks Korean ... and sign language.

As a POW in World War II, she and other religious people were arrested and held in prison, then sent on a Death March to a labor camp where she spent the years of the Korean War. After her release as a POW, she spent a year recuperating then returned to Korea, but to the South. Life was hard during the wars, including the Korean War from 1950-53, but even worse for the handicapped.

When she returned to Korea, Sister Caritas made contact with the deaf community again, and using her international and missionary connections, along with an exceptional optimism and exuberant personality, led a fundraising mission to buy some land and build a home for the deaf. Later the community built a school for deaf children, which now has about 300 students. They are a vibrant and thriving self-supporting community in what was originally the outskirts of Seoul but is now part of the sprawling urban landscape.

113

KYOPO

THE FOREIGN STUDENTS are holding a going-away party for Sunna, who is leaving to go to the States. She'll be at Mount Holyoke next year, too, so ours is a short-term goodbye. We take her to the restaurant at the Hyatt Hotel.

It seems that every person at her party is from a different country, though everyone is Korean, too, except me. In our group are students from Japan, Belgium, England, the U.S., Holland, Singapore, France, and maybe more. They all seem to be happy to be in Korea, which is great, because so many foreign-born Koreans have a hard time when they come here to study.

The ones who don't want to be here have no break between semesters back home, having given up whatever summer plans they might have had, being sent to Korea so they can study even more. Their parents hope they will learn to love the language and customs of their grandparents' homeland.

But instead of being encouraged for the effort to become more proficient, they are reprimanded by shopkeepers, taxi drivers, aunts, uncles, and family members in Korea, basically on all sides, for not having Korean mannerisms, for not speaking Korean well, and for dressing like the foreigners they also are.

While we are waiting to catch taxis home afterwards, we overhear one of these students say to another, "Don't you feel you are just spending your time here, waiting for the ride home?" What a contrast to me and my friends who love being in Korea—who will miss Korea when we go back to our home countries.

I am sorry that they don't seem to be welcomed home as much as I feel I am.

114

ID CHECKS

THE POLICE WERE CHECKING IDS at the main gate again yesterday, trying to make sure students supporters of Lim Soo-kyong—who is trying to return from North to South Korea through the DMZ negotiation village—could not access campus for protest. And the police hope to identify and arrest known activists, of course. The Korean Students played a small trick to get around the police.

KOREA HERALD   JULY 28, 1989

Radical students at major universities
barred from going to Panmunjom

Riot police force, ringing major college campuses and blocking main roads leading to Panmunjom, stopped radical students from welcoming dissident coed Lim Soo-kyong who tried to return from north Koran [sic] through the inter-Korean border village. yesterday.

A police spokesman said about 16,000 riot troops were deployed around universities in Seoul to keep student protesters from arching [sic] out of their campuses after holding rallies for welcoming Lim.

And under the **accompanying** photo of police and students at our main university gate is the following caption:

Riot police examine the identification cards of students in front of the school gate of Yonsei University in western Seoul, where radical students planned to rally to welcome Lim Soo-kyong's return from North Korea yesterday. The students held the rally at Seoul National University [instead] in a surprising move.

AUGUST 1989

115

SUCCESS

MY LITTLE STUDENT passed her reading test, and is accepted into second grade at the Foreign School! I am so excited when she tells me, and so is she, that we grab hands and dance in a circle. Her mother watches awkwardly, but she is happy, too. I told her how proud I am of her daughter, how she is such a little girl, but has worked so hard. In about three months she has gone from not knowing her alphabet to passing the exam to enter second grade.

Her mother hands me a prettily wrapped, small gift and tells me her daughter's success is all thanks to me. I hug my little student before she leaves, tears in my eyes, and whisper in her ear, "You are the one who did it!" Her mother takes her hand without a smile, they step into the back of her father's black sedan, and they are driven away.

I open the gift after they leave. A heavy gold necklace and matching earrings.

116

HOLDING ON

I'M DRIFTING OFF TO SLEEP to the familiar sound of the guys sitting on the bench that runs along the front of our rooms. They are drinking and talking, sometimes singing, their shadows silhouetted against the rice paper of my door. I'll miss them all so much when I go. The faces of my housemates and classmates run through my mind, bringing up memories. I want to hold onto each one: Flute Player, Salary Man, Younger Student, Youngest Guy, PhD Candidate, Little Brother, Sunna, JH, MJ, my Poker Partner, two new students replacing ones who have left, and the Student Monk. I think of memories together: telling ghost stories, running to catch a movie, laughing over beer, doing each other's homework, roasting dried squid, teasing each other, sharing coffee, exchanging little gifts, telling stories of family and memories of hometowns, conversations of demos and politics, going out for ice cream, poker, music, birthdays, crying and laughing together ... When will we ever see each other again?

117

LETTING GO

NOW I REALLY HAVE to go back to the States. This whole life here is ending so abruptly.

I have a last coffee with my housemates and move out of the temple room; give last classes to my students, meet one final time with my two Kims, who are dear to me now... I'm sitting on the rocky lookout on the mountain above the temple, the city below me, taking one more look to imprint it all in my mind.

My packing is finished and my parents have arranged to take me to the airport tomorrow. I wrap my notebooks in brown paper, my copy of the Manifesto nestled among them: I decide that the forbidden book will have to leave the country with me so it does not bring harm to anyone here. If found, I will do my best to explain, but I expect it is unlikely customs will check my bags on the way out.

Tomorrow I will wave from the airplane window until Seoul is lost in the clouds and mist. And everything that I have lived here will be like a story taken from a dream. Somehow I will fit into that other life back at Mount Holyoke as if it doesn't surprise me, and as if I don't expect to see a rice paper window when I wake up in the morning.

The air is clear, with only a light haze in the distance. From the mountain-top I say goodbye to the black roofed temples below, the gardens and fountains gathered under the mountain. The lush, green trees, a reddish-brown streak of the path running between them. I can see only a small piece of the cement wall near a clearing.

Beyond the foot of the mountain: the high-rise apartment buildings, and the offices and hotels of Seoul. Other mountains like this one rise like wooded islands out of the gray of the city, also shielding temples, mountain springs, and gray cliffs. Their sides are too steep for city buildings to cling to, so perhaps they will remain havens of quiet and mountain spirits ... Perhaps one day I can return to this one again.

118

KIMPO AIRPORT, SOUTH KOREA
CUSTOMS

TODAY I RETRACE MY STEPS through Kimpo airport, saying my final good-bye to Korea, piece by piece. Uniformed officials stamp my passport without question and send me through. I walk slowly past counters of cultural souvenirs I can now place in context, postcards of the life I'm leaving. The boarding area is crowded with excited tourists laden with carry-on bags, returning home. They are all talking at once, telling each other of the places they have visited and the neat things they have seen. I don't hear any mention of the demonstrations. I sit quietly, holding my bag full of memories, my journal, and the forbidden Manifesto: the only one who has nothing to say.

EPILOGUE

I N THE EARLY 1990s I returned to Korea to teach in the Foreign Language Institute at Yonsei University. I did not bring any forbidden books with me. I studied Taekwondo, played a part on a weekly TV show, and met my future husband. Again. And this time I stopped to talk with him when he said hello.

That is another story.

That's all.

ACKNOWLEDGMENTS

FIRST OF ALL, I have to thank my parents, Warren and Robin Hudson, for introducing me to Korea. Mom, I'm glad you got to read the original journal—and sorry that you aren't here anymore to hold my first published copy.

I offer a deep bow to the monks of Yongam-sa and Bongweon-sa who welcomed me and subtly watched over me, especially Beob-Hyeon Sunim. Appreciation to all my housemates and our raucous study sessions, birthdays, movies, meals, and camaraderie, without which this book could not have been written. And special affection to my Two Kims who became such good friends.

Thank you to the students and professors at Yonsei who shared stories as well as academics, and who welcomed me into their circles. Thank you to my professors at Mount Holyoke: Anne Jones, Jonathan Lipman, and my friends Deborah Frizzel and Anna Husson, who all saw the first draft of this story and encouraged me to revise, revise, and get it published.

Gratitude to so many friends, writing groups (especially Wordside) and my amazing family—especially my children and my many siblings and nieces!—who enjoyed later drafts and offered memories and feedback. Among them (don't be jealous!) I must single out Jen Keirans, librarian extraordinaire, for her professional touch and patience with all my questions. And of course, my most supportive husband, Alexander, who has encouraged me in all of my writing.

Special thanks to Professor Ron Dziwenka, Academic Editor, who offered advice and checked this manuscript for accuracy. I appreciate access to his extensive archive of Korean news articles which he gathered while also living in a monk's residence near Bongweon Temple as a graduate student at Yonsei University. That said, any remaining errors and opinions are my own responsibility.

And most recently, thanks to editor Lisa Jacob and publisher Steven Radecki at Paper Angel Press for asking so many good questions and bringing this book to light.

ABOUT THE AUTHOR

Christabel Choi's writing is inspired by treks over snowy mountain passes, tall ships on the high seas, transcontinental trains, and at least one circumnavigation of the globe. She grew up in rural Oregon in a close family hailing from four continents.

Christabel is settled in the San Francisco Bay Area with her husband, her father, and alternately one or all of her three children. Her office is filled with bows, arrows, horse tack, piles of paper and books, scattered projects, a dog, and a cat. Her life motto is to leave it better than she found it—except for her office, where maintenance is a noble enough goal.

YOU MIGHT ALSO ENJOY

BACK TO THE LAND IN SILICON VALLEY
Marlene Anne Bumgarner

When Marlene Bumgarner and her husband moved to a rural plot of land in 1973, she thought of herself as simply a young mother seeking an affordable and safe place in which to raise her child.

DAILY FRESH
Jory Post

In the summer of 2020, the final summer of his life, Jory Post gave himself an assignment: He would write one essay a day, inspired by whatever caught his eye and imagination.

DODGING PRAYERS AND BULLETS
Karen Beatty

A young girl prevails over poverty and religious bigotry to survive childhood abduction, a predatory theologian, family secrets, and the drug culture of the 1960s.

Available from Paper Angel Press in
hardcover, trade paperback, and digital editions
paperangelpress.com